EMPOWER YOURSELF RIGHT NOW

In the same series

Become Your Best Self Right Now
Make Your Life Extraordinary Right Now
Become Successful Right Now

EMPOWER YOURSELF RIGHT NOW

A MASTERCLASS FROM THE
SUPERGURUS

ALEPH

ALEPH BOOK COMPANY
An independent publishing firm
promoted by *Rupa Publications India*

First published in India in 2023
by Aleph Book Company
7/16 Ansari Road, Daryaganj
New Delhi 110 002

This anthology copyright © Aleph Book Company 2023.

Introduction copyright © Aleph Book Company 2023.

Copyright in individual excerpts vests with the copyright owners.

All rights reserved.

While every effort has been made to trace copyright holders and obtain permission, this has not been possible in all cases; any omissions brought to our attention will be remedied in future editions.

The views and opinions expressed in this book are those of the authors and the facts are as reported by them, which have been verified to the extent possible, and the publisher is not in any way liable for the same.

No part of this publication may be reproduced, transmitted, or stored in a retrieval system, in any form or by any means, without permission in writing from Aleph Book Company.

ISBN: 978-93-95853-98-9

1 3 5 7 9 10 8 6 4 2

Printed in India

This book is sold subject to the condition that it shall not, by way of trade or otherwise, be lent, resold, hired out, or otherwise circulated without the publisher's prior consent in any form of binding or cover other than that in which it is published.

Contents

Introduction ix

SECTION I
THE ROAD TO SUCCESS

1. Napoleon Hill: Think and Grow Rich 3
2. Neema Majumdar, Nandini Mirani, and Saloni Jhaveri: Finding Meaning in Life with the Bhagavad Gita 7
3. Dale Carnegie: How to Stop Worrying and Start Living 10
4. James Allen: From Poverty to Power: Or, the Realization of Prosperity 19
5. Henry Thomas Hamblin: Within You Is the Power 27
6. Kahlil Gibran: The Prophet 34
7. Arnold Bennett: How to Live on Twenty-four Hours a Day 36

SECTION II
GETTING THE BEST OUT OF YOURSELF

8. Joseph Murphy: The Power of Your
   Subconscious Mind 43
9. Orison Swett Marden: Cheerfulness as a
   Life Power 46
10. Kahlil Gibran: The Prophet 54
11. James Allen: Above Life's Turmoil 56
12. Neema Majumdar, Nandini Mirani, and
    Saloni Jhaveri: Finding Meaning in Life
    with the Bhagavad Gita 60
13. Arnold Bennett: How to Live on
    Twenty-four Hours a Day 63
14. Arthur Schopenhauer: Counsels and Maxims ... 67

SECTION III
FINDING INNER STRENGTH

15. Napoleon Hill: Think and Grow Rich 73
16. Neema Majumdar, Nandini Mirani,
    and Saloni Jhaveri: Finding Meaning in
    Life with the Bhagavad Gita 76
17. Joseph Murphy: The Power of Your Subconscious
    Mind 79
18. Kahlil Gibran: The Prophet 83
19. James Allen: How Pain Leads to Knowledge
    and Power 85

20. Dale Carnegie: How to Stop Worrying
    and Start Living — 89
21. Henry Thomas Hamblin: Within You Is the Power — 95

SECTION IV
MAKING USE OF OPPORTUNITIES

22. Ralph Waldo Emerson: Circles — 105
23. James Allen: Out from the Heart — 110
24. Orison Swett Marden: The Victorious Attitude — 114
25. Neema Majumdar, Nandini Mirani, and Saloni Jhaveri: Finding Meaning in Life with the Bhagavad Gita — 121
26. Joseph Murphy: The Power of Your Subconscious Mind — 125
27. William George Jordan: The Majesty of Calmness — 129
28. Kahlil Gibran: The Prophet — 137

Notes on Contributors — 139

Light, oh where is the light! Kindle it with the burning fire of desire! It thunders and the wind rushes screaming through the void. The night is black as a black stone. Let not the hours pass by in the dark. Kindle the lamp of love with thy life.

–*Gitanjali*, Rabindranath Tagore

Introduction

The world we inhabit today is marked by constant flux and contradictions, brimming with material desires that can be fulfilled with a single click or a tap of a button. However, this also happens to be a time of unprecedented emotional complexities, a time of endless inner battles and external pressures that often make us question our self-worth. Despite being surrounded by abundant opportunities, we are bound to encounter unfavourable situations that seem out of our control, and they make it difficult for us to realize our potential and make the most of what life has to offer. These roadblocks cloud our vision, make our dreams appear hazy, and we stumble on the path to fulfilment. The chasm between one's true self and what is simply projected to conform to the norm continues to widen and there creeps in patterns and actions that do more harm than good in our pursuit of success.

In such a scenario, an individual desires two things: their pain to be acknowledged and to be guided away from self-imposed shackles and towards the direction of joy. And this is where supergurus make their entrance. These immensely charismatic, wise, and learned men and women have spent their lives exploring existential questions integral to the human experience, and in the process, have discovered secrets that have proved to be tremendously beneficial for millions seeking illumination and solace. The supergurus understand how success, fulfilment, and progress mean different things to different people. So instead of treating such ideas as monolithic blocks and pushing one and all towards an identical destination, their extensive experience in the field of psychological development ensures that their profound insights can be moulded to fit each person's reality and bring about radical empowerment in a way that retains individuality and helps people gain joy and equilibrium. They don't speak in abstractions or offer solutions that are out of reach for the common man and woman. Their answers are easy to implement, perceptive, and above all, deeply considerate of the vast spectrum of emotional upheavals that one may face during their lifetime.

Empower Yourself Right Now brings together several powerful insights from some of the greatest supergurus who hail from every corner of the world and have collectively sold over a hundred million copies of their books. They have topped bestseller lists, been extensively translated, and touched the lives of billions of people. In this anthology, their essential wisdom (in the form of excerpts from their best-known books or most famous lessons) is being made available to readers in a conjoint volume. As most of the material in this book is gleaned from previously published titles now in the public domain, the text has not been standardized. Besides this introduction and the introduction to each excerpt, all the material sourced from books is reproduced as it first appeared.

INTRODUCTION

The book has four sections, and each section contains seven chapters—think of them as a friend for every day of the week. A friend who shows you a new source of happiness. A friend who offers a fresh perspective on an age-old problem. A friend who will be your guide as you take sure and steady steps towards empowerment in the truest sense of the term—be it in your professional life, in your path to spiritual development, or in areas of personal growth. And how do you approach the book? The answer is any way you wish to. The chapters can be read in the sequence in which they appear or selected at random. The book is short enough to finish in a single sitting. Alternatively, you can consider incorporating it into your routine, reading one chapter a day and then reflecting upon the ideas they contain. No matter which way you choose, the key is to internalize its contents in a way it resonates with you. Utilize these enlightened words to begin a conversation in which you attempt to revisit your life through a transformed lens. By personalizing your relationship with this book and its teachings, you are sure to tackle challenges successfully, unlock your potential, and become the happiest version of yourself. Your dream is a step away.

—The Editors

SECTION I

THE ROAD TO SUCCESS

.1.

Napoleon Hill

Think and Grow Rich

An international sensation in the personal development genre, Think and Grow Rich has sold tens of millions of copies ever since its publication in 1937. In this extract, the author emphasizes intense desire as the first step to making the most of opportunities that are sure to bring everlasting success.

~

Awake, arise, and assert yourself, you dreamers of the world. Your star is now in the ascendency. The world depression brought the opportunity you have been waiting for. It taught people humility, tolerance, and open-mindedness.

The world is filled with an abundance of OPPORTUNITY which the dreamers of the past never knew.

A BURNING DESIRE TO BE, AND TO DO is the starting point from which the dreamer must take off. Dreams are not born of indifference, laziness, or lack of ambition.

The world no longer scoffs at the dreamer, nor calls him impractical. If you think it does, take a trip to Tennessee, and witness what a dreamer president has done in the way of harnessing, and using the great water power of America. A score of years ago, such a dream would have seemed like madness.

You have been disappointed, you have undergone defeat during the depression, you have felt the great heart within you crushed until it bled. Take courage, for these experiences have tempered the spiritual metal of which you are made—they are assets of incomparable value.

Remember, too, that all who succeed in life get off to a bad start, and pass through many heartbreaking struggles before they 'arrive'. The turning point in the lives of those who succeed usually comes at the moment of some crisis, through which they are introduced to their 'other selves'.

John Bunyan wrote the *Pilgrim's Progress*, which is among the finest of all English literature, after he had been confined in prison and sorely punished, because of his views on the subject of religion.

O. Henry discovered the genius which slept within his brain, after he had met with great misfortune, and was confined in a prison cell, in Columbus, Ohio. Being FORCED, through misfortune, to become acquainted with his "other self," and to use his IMAGINATION, he discovered himself to be a great author instead of a miserable criminal and outcast. Strange and varied are the ways of life, and stranger still are the ways of Infinite Intelligence, through which men are sometimes forced to undergo all sorts of punishment before discovering their own brains, and their own capacity to create useful ideas through imagination.

Edison, the world's greatest inventor and scientist, was a 'tramp' telegraph operator, he failed innumerable times before he was driven, finally, to the discovery of the genius which slept within his brain.

Charles Dickens began by pasting labels on blacking pots. The tragedy of his first love penetrated the depths of his soul and converted him into one of the world's truly great authors. That tragedy produced, first, *David Copperfield*, then a succession of other works that made this a richer and better world for all who read his books. Disappointment over love affairs, generally has the effect of driving men to drink, and women to ruin; and this is because most people never learn the art of transmuting their strongest emotions into dreams of a constructive nature.

Helen Keller became deaf, dumb, and blind shortly after birth. Despite her greatest misfortune, she has written her name indelibly in the pages of the history of the great. Her entire life has served as evidence that no one ever is defeated until defeat has been accepted as a reality.

Robert Burns was an illiterate country lad, he was cursed by poverty and grew up to be a drunkard in the bargain. The world was made better for his having lived, because he clothed beautiful thoughts in poetry, and thereby plucked a thorn and planted a rose in its place.

Booker T. Washington was born in slavery, handicapped by race and colour. Because he was tolerant, had an open mind at all times, on all subjects, and was a DREAMER, he left his impress for good on an entire race.

Beethoven was deaf, Milton was blind, but their names will last as long as time endures because they dreamed and translated their dreams into organized thought.

Kindle anew in your mind the fire of hope, faith,

courage, and tolerance. Let Emerson state the thought in these words, 'Every proverb, every book, every byword that belongs to thee for aid and comfort shall surely come home through open or winding passages. Every friend whom not thy fantastic will, but the great and tender soul in thee craveth, shall lock thee in his embrace.'

There is a difference between WISHING for a thing and being READY to receive it. No one is ready for a thing until he believes he can acquire it. The state of mind must be BELIEF, not mere hope or wish. Open-mindedness is essential for belief. Closed minds do not inspire faith, courage, and belief.

Remember, no more effort is required to aim high in life, to demand abundance and prosperity than is required to accept misery and poverty. A great poet has correctly stated this universal truth through these lines:

*'I bargained with Life for a penny,
And Life would pay no more,
However I begged at evening
When I counted my scanty store.*

*For Life is a just employer,
He gives you what you ask,
But once you have set the wages,
Why, you must bear the task.*

*I worked for a menial's hire,
Only to learn, dismayed,
That any wage I had asked of Life,
Life would have willingly paid.'*

.2.

Neema Majumdar, Nandini Mirani, and Saloni Jhaveri

Finding Meaning in Life with the Bhagavad Gita

The Bhagavad Gita, one of the greatest spiritual texts in the world, is a 700-verse narrative discourse in the Bhishma Parva of the epic Mahabharata. In Verse 9, Lord Krishna explains to Arjuna the profound relationship of action with self-knowledge.

~

The Goal of Action

व्यवसायात्मिका बुद्धिरेकेह कुरुनन्दन।
बहुशाखा ह्यनन्ताश्च बुद्धयोऽव्यवसायिनाम् ॥2-41॥

*vyavasāyātmikā buddhirekeha kurunandana
bahuśākhā hyanantāśca buddhayo'vyavasāyinām*

With reference to this (moksha), Arjuna, the descendant of Kurus! There is a single, well-ascertained understanding. The notions of those who lack discrimination are many branched and innumerable indeed. (2.41)

~

Only the knowledge that 'I' am already complete will provide lasting fulfilment. However, action is vital to prepare oneself for this knowledge even though action is intrinsically incapable of providing fulfilment. Any action which is inherently limited and finite, produces a result which is also limited and hence is not capable of providing us with freedom from limitations. For example, no matter how much wealth a person amasses, it cannot provide him freedom from physical or psychological suffering, nor is there a guarantee that he can protect his wealth for a lifetime. Even if he manages to do so, he must still part with it when his time on earth is over.

Action, however, has a critical role to play in the journey towards ultimate fulfilment. By performing action as a karma yogi, we remove the afflictions from which we suffer—such as ethical dilemmas, emotional quandaries, or loss of perspective. We are not detached or without desire—rather, we enthusiastically engage with life, and express and act upon desires responsibly. We learn to accept the results of actions with equanimity. Living a life of karma yoga purifies our mind, helps us master our emotions, and transforms various aspects of our daily life.

How is a normal ethical person different from a karma yogi? In spite of being ethical in action, a person can be pursuing fulfilment through never-ending goals like wealth, power, security, or fame. However, for a karma yogi, the goal of life is to understand the reality of his true nature, while being fully engaged in action with the right attitude.

Lord Krishna says that unless the goal of life is clear, as one of self-discovery and self-growth, we continue to search for fulfilment in numerous so-called material and spiritual pursuits which are endless in nature.

.3.

Dale Carnegie

How to Stop Worrying and Start Living

Dale Carnegie's classic bestseller is one of the most widely-read self-help books in the world. In this lesson, he demonstrates easy-to-implement pointers on how to evaluate a roadblock, formulate steps for its resolution, and achieve calm in the face of chaos.

~

We must equip ourselves to deal with different kinds of worries by learning the three basic steps of problem analysis. The three steps are:

- Get the facts.
- Analyse the facts.
- Arrive at a decision, and then act on that decision.

Obvious stuff? Yes, Aristotle taught it—and used it. And you and I must use it too if we are going to solve the problems that are harassing us and turning our days and nights into veritable hells.

Let's take the first rule: get the facts. Why is it so important to get the facts? Because unless we have the facts we can't possibly even attempt to solve our problem intelligently. Without the facts, all we can do is stew around in confusion. My idea? No, that was the idea of the late Herbert E. Hawkes, Dean of Columbia College, Columbia University, for twenty-two years. He had helped two hundred thousand students solve their worry problems, and he told me that 'confusion is the chief cause of worry'. He put it this way—he said: 'Half the worry in the world is caused by people trying to make decisions before they have sufficient knowledge on which to base a decision. For example, if I have a problem which has to be faced at three o'clock next Tuesday, I refuse even to try to make a decision about it until next Tuesday arrives. In the meantime, I concentrate on getting all the facts that bear on the problem. I don't worry. I don't agonise over my problem. I don't lose any sleep. I simply concentrate on getting the facts. And by the time Tuesday rolls around, if I've got all the facts, the problem usually solves itself!'

I asked Dean Hawkes if this meant he had licked worry entirely. 'Yes,' he said, 'I think I can honestly say that my live is now almost totally devoid of worry. I have found,' he went on, 'that if a man will devote his time to securing facts in an impartial, objective way, his worries usually evaporate in the light of knowledge.'

But what do most of us do? If we bother with facts at all and Thomas Edison said in all seriousness: 'There is no expedient to which a man will not resort to avoid the labour of thinking'—if we bother with facts at all, we hunt like bird dogs after the facts that bolster up what we already think—and ignore all the others! We want only the facts that justify our acts—the facts that fit in conveniently with our wishful thinking and justify our preconceived prejudices!

Is it any wonder, then, that we find it so hard to get at the answers to our problems? Wouldn't we have the same trouble trying to solve a second—grade arithmetic problem, if we went ahead on the assumption that two plus two equals five? Yet there are a lot of people in this world who make life a hell for themselves and others by insisting that two plus two equals five—or maybe five hundred!

What can we do about it? We have to keep our emotions out of our thinking; and, as Dean Hawkes put it, we must secure the facts in 'an impartial, objective' manner. That is not an easy task when we are worried. When we are worried, our emotions are riding high. But here are two ideas that I have found helpful when trying to step aside from my problems, in order to see the facts in a clear, objective manner.

When trying to get the facts, I pretend that I am collecting this information not for myself, but for some other person. This helps me to take a cold, impartial view of the evidence. This helps me eliminate my emotions.

While trying to collect the facts about the problem that is worrying me, I sometimes pretend that I am a lawyer preparing to argue the other side of the issue. In other words, I try to get all the facts against myself—all the facts that are damaging to my wishes, all the facts I don't like to face. Then I write down both my side of the case and the other side of the case—and I generally find that the truth lies somewhere in between these two extremities. Here is the point I am trying to make. Neither you nor I nor Einstein nor the Supreme Court of the United States is brilliant enough to reach an intelligent decision on any problem without first getting the facts. Thomas Edison knew that. At the time of his death, he had two thousand five hundred notebooks filled with facts about the problems he was facing. So Rule 1 for solving our problems is: *Get the facts.* Let's do what Dean Hawkes did: let's not even attempt to solve our problems without first collecting all the facts in an impartial manner.

However, getting all the facts in the world won't do us any good until we analyse them and interpret them. I have found from costly experience that it is much easier to analyse the facts after writing them. In fact, merely writing the facts on a piece of paper and stating our problem clearly goes a long way toward helping us to reach a sensible decision. As Charles Kettering puts it: 'A problem well stated is a problem half solved.'

Let me show you all this as it works out in practice. Since the Chinese say one picture is worth ten thousand words, suppose I show you a picture of how one man put exactly what we are talking about into concrete action.

Let's take the case of Galen Litchfield—a man I have known for several years; one of the most successful American business men in the Far East. Mr. Litchfield was in China in 1942, when the Japanese invaded Shanghai. And here is his story as he told it to me while a guest in my home:

'Shortly after the Japs took Pearl Harbour,' Galen Litchfield began, 'they came swarming into Shanghai. I was the manager of the Asia Life Insurance Company in Shanghai. They sent us an "army liquidator"—he was really an admiral— and gave me orders to assist this man in liquidating our assets. I didn't have any choice in the matter. I could cooperate—or else. And the "or else" was certain death.

I went through the motions of doing what I was told, because I had no alternative. But there was one block of securities, worth $750,000, which I left off the list I gave to the admiral. I left that block of securities off the list because they belonged to our Hong Kong organisation and had nothing to do with the Shanghai assets. All the same, I feared I might be in hot water if the Japs found out what I had done. And they soon found out.

I wasn't in the office when the discovery was made, but my head accountant was there. He told me that the Jap admiral flew into a rage, and stamped and swore, and called me a thief and a traitor! I had defied the Japanese Army! I knew what that meant. I would be thrown into the Bridge House! The Bridge House was the torture chamber of the Japanese Gestapo! I had personal friends who had killed themselves rather than be taken to that prison. I had other friends who had died in that place after ten days of questioning and torture. Now I was slated for the Bridge House myself! What did I do? I heard the news on Sunday afternoon. I suppose I should have been terrified. And I would have been terrified if I hadn't had a definite technique for solving my problems. For years, whenever I was worried I had always gone to my typewriter and written down two questions—and the answers to these questions:

1. ***What am I worrying about?***
2. ***What can I do about it?***

I used to try to answer those questions without writing them down. But I stopped that years ago. I found that writing down both the questions and the answers clarifies my thinking.

So, that Sunday afternoon, I went directly to my room at the Shanghai Y. M. C. A. and got out my typewriter. I wrote: 1. *What am I worrying about?*

I am afraid I will be thrown into the Bridge house tomorrow morning. Then I typed out the second question: 2. *What can I do about it?* I spent hours thinking out and writing down the four courses of action I could take—and what the probable consequence of each action would be.

1. I can try to explain this to the Japanese admiral. But he 'no speak English'. If I try to explain to him through an interpreter, I may stir him up again. That might mean death, for he is cruel, would rather dump me in the Bridge House than bother talking about it.
2. I can try to escape. Impossible. They keep track of me all the time. I have to check in and out of my room at the Y. M. C. A. If I try to escape, I'll probably be captured and shot.
3. I can stay here in my room and not go near the office again. If I do, the Japanese admiral will be suspicious, will probably send soldiers to get me and throw me into the Bridge House without giving me a chance to say a word.

4. I can go down to the office as usual on Monday morning. If I do, there is a chance that the Japanese admiral may be so busy that he will not think of what I did. Even if he does think of it, he may have cooled off and may not bother me. If this happens, I am all right. Even if he does bother me, I'll still have a chance to try to explain to him. So, going down to the office as usual on Monday morning, and acting as if nothing had gone wrong gives me two chances to escape the Bridge House. As soon as I thought it all out and decided to accept the fourth plan—to go down to the office as usual on Monday morning—I felt immensely relieved.

When I entered the office the next morning, the Japanese admiral sat there with a cigarette dangling from his mouth. He glared at me as he always did; and said nothing. Six weeks later—thank God—he went back to Tokyo and my worries were ended.

As I have already said, I probably saved my life by sitting down that Sunday afternoon and writing out all the various steps I could take and then writing down the probable consequences of each step and calmly coming to a decision. If I hadn't done that, I might have floundered and hesitated and done the wrong thing on the spur of the moment. If I hadn't thought out my problem and come to a decision, I would have been frantic with worry all Sunday afternoon. I wouldn't have slept that night. I would have gone down to the office Monday morning with a harassed and worried look, and that alone might have aroused the suspicion of the Japanese admiral and spurred him to act.

Experience has proved to me, time after time, the enormous value of arriving at a decision. It is the failure to arrive at a fixed purpose, the inability to stop going round and round in maddening circles, that drives men to nervous breakdowns and living hells. I find that fifty per cent of my worries vanish once I arrive at a clear, definite decision; and another forty per cent usually vanishes once I start to carry out that decision.'

Why is Galen Litchfield's method so superb? Because it is efficient, concrete, and goes directly to the heart of the problem. On top of all that, it is climaxed by the third and indispensable rule: do something about it. Unless we carry out our action, all our fact-finding and analysis is whistling upwind—it's a sheer waste of energy.

William James said this: 'When once a decision is reached and execution is the order of the day, dismiss absolutely all responsibility and care about the outcome.' In this case, William James undoubtedly used the word 'care' as a synonym for 'anxiety'. He meant—once you have made a careful decision based on facts, *go* into action. Don't stop to reconsider. Don't begin to hesitate worry and retrace your steps. Don't lose yourself in self-doubting which begets other doubts. Don't keep looking back over your shoulder. I once asked Waite Phillips, one of Oklahoma's most prominent oil men, how he carried out decisions. He replied: 'I find that to keep thinking about our problems beyond a certain point is bound to create confusion and worry. There comes a time when any more investigation and thinking are harmful.'

There comes a time when we must decide and act and never look back. Why don't you employ Galen Litchfield's technique to one of your worries right now?

Question No. 1. What am I worrying about?
Question No. 2. What can I do about it?
Question No. 3. Here is what I am going to do about it.
Question No. 4. When am I going to start doing it?

.4.

James Allen

From Poverty to Power:
Or, the Realization of Prosperity

James Allen, a renowned British thinker and writer, wrote several inspirational tracts and poems, From Poverty to Power: Or, the Realization of Prosperity *being his debut book. In this section, the author teaches us the secret of health, success, and power.*

~

We all remember with what intense delight, as children, we listened to the never tiring fairy-tale. How eagerly we followed the fluctuating fortunes of the good boy or girl, ever protected, in the hour of crisis, from the evil machinations of the scheming witch, the cruel giant, or the wicked king. And our little hearts never faltered for the fate of the hero or heroine, nor did we doubt their ultimate triumph over all their enemies, for we knew that the fairies were infallible and that they would never desert those who had consecrated themselves to the good and the true. And what unspeakable joy pulsated within us when the Fairy-Queen, bringing all her magic to bear at the critical moment, scattered all the darkness and trouble, and granted them the complete satisfaction of all their hopes, and they were 'happy ever after'.

With the accumulating years, and an ever-increasing intimacy with the so-called 'realities' of life, our beautiful fairy-world became obliterated, and its wonderful inhabitants were relegated, in the archives of memory, to the shadowy and unreal. And we thought we were wise and strong in thus leaving for ever the land of childish dreams, but as we re-become little children in the wondrous world of wisdom, we shall return again to the inspiring dreams of childhood and find that they are, after all, realities.

The fairy-folk, so small and nearly always invisible, yet possessed of an all-conquering and magical power, who bestow upon the good, health, wealth, and happiness, along with all the gifts of nature in lavish profusion, start again into reality and become immortalized in the soul-realm of him who, by growth in wisdom, has entered into a knowledge of the power of thought, and the laws which govern the inner world of being. To him the fairies live again as thought-people, thought-messengers, thought powers working in harmony with the over-ruling Good. And they who, day by day, endeavour to harmonize their hearts with the heart of the Supreme Good, do in reality acquire true health, wealth, and happiness.

There is no protection to compare with goodness, and by 'goodness' I do not mean a mere outward conformity to the rules of morality; I mean pure thought, noble aspiration, unselfish love, and freedom from vainglory. To dwell continually in good thoughts, is to throw around oneself a psychic atmosphere of sweetness and power which leaves its impress upon all who come in contact with it. As the rising sun puts to rout the helpless shadows, so are all the impotent forces of evil put to flight by the searching rays of positive thought which shine forth from a heart made strong in purity and faith.

Where there is sterling faith and uncompromising purity there is health, there is success, there is power. In such a one, disease, failure, and disaster can find no lodgment, for there is nothing on which they can feed. Even physical conditions are largely determined by mental states, and to this truth the scientific world is rapidly being drawn.

The old, materialistic belief that a man is what his body makes him, is rapidly passing away, and is being replaced by the inspiring belief that man is superior to his body and that his body is what he makes it by the power of thought. Men everywhere are ceasing to believe that a man is despairing because he is dyspeptic, and are coming to understand that he is dyspeptic because he is despairing, and in the near future, the fact that all disease has its origin in the mind will become common knowledge. There is no evil in the universe but has its root and origin in the mind, and sin, sickness, sorrow, and affliction do not, in reality, belong to the universal order, are not inherent in the nature of things, but are the direct outcome of our ignorance of the right relations of things.

According to tradition, there once lived, in India, a school of philosophers who led a life of such absolute purity and simplicity that they commonly reached the age of one hundred and fifty years, and to fall sick was looked upon by them as an unpardonable disgrace, for it was considered to indicate a violation of law. The sooner we realize and acknowledge that sickness, far from being the arbitrary visitation of an offended God, or the test of an unwise Providence, is the result of our own error or sin, the sooner shall we enter upon the highway of health. Disease comes to those who attract it, to those whose minds and bodies are receptive to it, and flees from those whose strong, pure, and positive thought-sphere generates healing and life-giving currents.

If you are given to anger, worry, jealousy, greed, or any other inharmonious state of mind, and expect perfect physical health, you are expecting the impossible, for you are continually sowing the seeds of disease in your mind. Such conditions of mind are carefully shunned by the wise man, for he knows them to be far more dangerous than a bad drain or an infected house.

If you would be free from all physical aches and pains, and would enjoy perfect physical harmony, then put your mind in order, and harmonize your thoughts. Think joyful thoughts; think loving thoughts; let the elixir of goodwill course through your veins, and you will need no other medicine. Put away your jealousies, your suspicions, your worries, your hatreds, your selfish indulgences, and you will put away your dyspepsia, your biliousness, your nervousness and aching joints. If you will persist in clinging to these debilitating and demoralizing habits of mind, then do not complain when your body is laid low with sickness.

The following story illustrates the close relation that exists between habits of mind and bodily conditions. A certain man was afflicted with a painful disease, and he tried one physician after another, but all to no purpose. He then visited towns which were famous for their curative waters, and after having bathed in them all, his disease was more painful than ever.

One night he dreamed that a Presence came to him and said, 'Brother, hast thou tried all the means of cure?' and he replied, 'I have tried all.' 'Nay,' said the Presence, 'come with me, and I will show thee a healing bath which has escaped thy notice.'

The afflicted man followed, and the Presence led him to a clear pool of water, and said, 'Plunge thyself in this water and thou shalt surely recover,' and thereupon vanished.

The man plunged into the water, and on coming out, lo! his disease had left him, and at the same moment he saw written above the pool the word 'Renounce.' Upon waking, the fall meaning of his dream flashed across his mind and looking within he discovered that he had, all along, been a victim to a sinful indulgence, and he vowed that he would renounce it for ever.

He carried out his vow, and from that day his affliction began to leave him, and in a short time, he was completely restored to health. Many people complain that they have broken down through over-work. In the majority of such cases, the breakdown is more frequently the result of foolishly wasted energy.

If you would secure health you must learn to work without friction. To become anxious or excited, or to worry over needless details is to invite a breakdown. Work, whether of brain or body, is beneficial and health-giving, and the man who can work with a steady and calm persistency, freed from all anxiety and worry, and with his mind utterly oblivious to all but the work he has in hand, will not only accomplish far more than the man who is always hurried and anxious, but he will retain his health, a boon which the other quickly forfeits.

True health and true success go together, for they are inseparably intertwined in the thought-realm. As mental harmony produces bodily health, so it also leads to a harmonious sequence in the actual working out of one's plans. Order your thoughts and you will order your life. Pour the oil of tranquillity upon the turbulent waters of the passions and prejudices, and the tempests of misfortune, howsoever they may threaten, will be powerless to wreck the barque of your soul, as it threads its way across the ocean of life.

And if that barque be piloted by a cheerful and never-failing faith its course will be doubly sure, and many perils will pass it by which would other-wise attack it. By the power of faith, every enduring work is accomplished. Faith in the Supreme; faith in the over-ruling Law; faith in your work, and in your power to accomplish that work, -here is the rock upon which you must build if you would achieve, if you would stand and not fall.

To follow, under all circumstances, the highest promptings within you; to be always true to the divine self; to rely upon the inward Light, the inward Voice, and to pursue your purpose with a fearless and restful heart, believing that the future will yield unto you the seed of every thought and effort; knowing that the laws of the universe can never fail and that your own will come back to you with mathematical exactitude, this is faith and the living of faith.

By the power of such a faith, the dark waters of uncertainty are divided, every mountain of difficulty crumbles away, and the believing soul passes on unharmed. Strive, O reader! to acquire, above everything, the priceless possession of this dauntless faith, for it is the talisman of happiness, of success, of peace, of power, of all that makes life great and superior to suffering.

Build upon such a faith, and you build upon the Rock of the Eternal, and with the materials of the Eternal, and the structure that you erect will never be dissolved, for it will transcend all the accumulations of material luxuries and riches, the end of which is dust.

Whether you are hurled into the depths of sorrow or lifted upon the heights of joy, ever retain your hold upon this faith, ever return to it as your rock of refuge, and keep your feet firmly planted upon its immortal and immovable base. Centred in such a faith, you will become possessed of such a spiritual strength as will shatter, like so many toys of glass, all the forces of evil that are hurled against you, and you will achieve success such as the mere striver after worldly gain can never know or even dream of. 'If ye have faith, and doubt not, ye shall not only do this, ... but if ye shall say unto this mountain, be thou removed and be thou cast into the sea, it shall be done.'

There are those today, men and women tabernacled in flesh and blood, who have realized this faith, who live in it and by it, day by day, and who, having put it to the uttermost test, have entered into the possession of its glory and peace. Such have sent out the word of command, and the mountains of sorrow and disappointment, of mental weariness and physical pain have passed from them, and have been cast into the sea of oblivion. If you will become possessed of this faith you will not need to trouble about your success or failure, and success will come. You will not need to become anxious about results, but will work joyfully and peacefully, knowing that right thoughts and right efforts will inevitably bring about right results.

.5.

Henry Thomas Hamblin

Within You Is the Power

An English mystic and pioneer of the New Thought Movement, Henry Thomas Hamblin wrote extensively on nurturing the mind and spirit and manifesting positivity. In this section, he reveals the true meaning of achieving success and how to sustain it through one's lifetime.

~

What is meant here by success is the achievement of something worthwhile, that shall make the world better and richer, and add something to the common good. Our sphere in life may be very humble, but if we overcome our own weaknesses, help others along life's pathway, and do our daily work better than we need, our life cannot be other than successful. If, at the end of our life, we can be thankful for it, realizing that we have made the best possible use of it, we have achieved real success.

Success, to the unillumined, may mean the accumulation of wealth and the winning of fame. Yet those who give up their lives to the acquirement of these things are the greatest failures in life. They gain wealth, it is true, but they find that their money can buy only those things that bring no satisfaction: that it cannot purchase for them any of the things which are really worth having. Success of this hollow kind can be won but at too great a price. The greatest Teacher of all once said: 'For what shall it profit man, if he shall gain the whole world and lose his own soul? What does it profit a man if he "gets on" at the cost of happiness, health, joy of living, domestic life, and the ability to appreciate Nature's beauties and simple pleasures?'

Yet man must be a striver. He must be for ever seeking better things and to express himself more perfectly. One who drifts through life, making no effort to rise to better things, is not worthy of the name of a citizen. Man, if he is to be worthy of the name, must be for ever striving, overcoming, rising. Failure in life is always due to weakness of character. It is only strong characters who can resist the buffetings of life and overcome its difficulties. The man who would make his life worthy of respect and who would rise to high achievement and service, will be confronted by difficulty at every turn. This is as it should be, for it weeds out the weaklings and unworthy aspirants, and awards the spoils to those who exhibit faith, courage, steadfastness, patience, perseverance, persistence, cheerfulness, and strength of character, generally. Success, especially material success, is not, in itself, of much benefit to the one who wins it. It does not satisfy for long, but it is valuable in other ways. For instance, success, based on service, is a benefit to the community. If, it were not for successful people of this type the ordinary man in the rut would have a bad time. Also, winning success builds up character. One who would be successful in the battle of life must be prepared to be tested and tried in every possible way. One who survives them all is built up in character in almost every direction. Even in his success, however, he will be tempted and tried. One who is engaged in the harsh struggle of business, or who takes part in public life, may, if he does not watch himself very carefully, become hard and callous. Of all failures, this is probably the worst. One who succeeds in other directions and becomes a "hard man," is, after all, a sorry failure.

Again, people of the successful, striving, climbing type, are tempted far more than those who are afraid to venture and who remain in the valley of mediocrity. This is true, not only of those who seek to climb the steep path of spiritual attainment, but also of those who are successful in mundane affairs. In each case, they have placed in their keeping great powers and influence such as the ordinary man little dreams of. This is a grave responsibility, for if these powers are used for self-aggrandisement the results are disastrous. Thus, those who climb, are beset on all sides by temptations of a very subtle kind, which, if yielded to, will ruin the life and do grave injury to the soul.

Life is a continual battle. To the ordinary person it is generally a fight with circumstances and the ordinary difficulties of life which are very important in his eyes. The more advanced soul is not troubled much by these things—he rises above them—but he is tempted and tried to a much greater degree and in a far more subtle manner. Those who think that by following a certain 'cult' or 'ism', they will be able to have an uneventful walk through life are merely deluding themselves. As he learns to overcome the difficulties of life which baffle the ordinary individual, he will be tempted and tried in other and more subtle ways. This is because life is not for mere passing pleasure, but is for the building up of character, through experience. Therefore, one who would succeed must be strong, and wise and patient. Those who aspire to make their lives really worthwhile: who desire to serve their fellows more perfectly: who want to build up character through experience and overcome all their weaknesses, inherited or otherwise, must look within for power and wisdom.

It must be pointed out, however, that man must not use his spiritual powers for selfish purposes and self-aggrandizement. There is an immutable law, which has been known to the inner teaching all through the ages, that forbids the use of spiritual powers for the creation of wealth or even of daily bread. Jesus was subject to the same spiritual law and was tempted exactly in the same way as we. The tempter said: 'Command this stone that it be made bread.' If Christ had turned the stone into bread, He would have failed in His great mission, but He knew the law. There are thousands of people to-day who are trying, not only to turn, by the misuse of their spiritual powers, stones into bread, but also into motor cars, fat bank balances and lands and houses. Such are heading to disaster, for they are working against the combined Spiritual Power of the Universe. The Enemy of Souls offers those who have learned to tap the inexhaustible Power of the Universe, and who have discovered that they are sons of God, wealth, power, pomp, the applause of men—the glittering things that perish—if only they will misuse their God-given power. Like Jesus, they must refuse. They must put service before self, and give instead of grasping.

Thousands are being taught to-day to force their human will upon life and to use occult powers for the acquisition of wealth and power. They are taught to enter the Silence and demand 'what they want'. 'How to get what you want' is the slogan of these modern teachers. Not merit, not service, not giving, but demanding, compelling by human will-power and by the use of occult forces. This is another device of the Enemy of Souls, and it is taking tens of thousands of seekers for Truth out of the Path. This subject is dealt with more fully in a separate chapter.

If, however, man's ambition is to serve and to give, instead of to grasp and to grab: if, also, he seeks success through merit and not through the misuse of his spiritual powers, he can go forward and the Power will go with him and will help him. When once the Power has been aroused, man must cease all purely selfish striving, although, of course, there will still be much selfishness in his motive. He must seek his success through service and through following noble aims: through merit and fair exchange, instead of trying to wring success from life, no matter who may suffer thereby.

Further, when this Power has been brought into expression it must only be used in love, for if it is used otherwise it will destroy the user. Again, the Power must not be used by the finite human will, but an endeavour must be made to find what the Will of the Whole is and to work in harmony with it.

Behind each life is the Divine Will and Purpose. Each life is perfect as it is imaged in the Universal Mind. The highest success, indeed, the only true success, is to live life according to the great Cosmic Purpose, or, in other words, as it is imaged in the One Mind.

Do not imagine, however, that it is the Will of the Universal Mind that man should be a failure or lacking in achievement. Far from it, for we have only to contemplate the Universe to see that the Infinite Mind is for ever achieving and that it never fails. Man, too, must succeed, but let him mix wisdom with his ambition, and work for the benefit of the Whole, rather than for any purely selfish purpose.

It is natural for man to 'get on' in life, to a moderate extent. In order to 'get on' he must become more efficient, and thus serve life and his fellows better. Therefore, there is no harm in success of this kind. It is natural and laudable also for one in poor and unlovely surroundings to have an ambition to raise himself to better circumstances. It is only right that he should desire to make life brighter and better for his wife and family. So long as he indulges in ambition wisely, and if he seeks success through better service to his fellows, his is a laudable purpose. If, however, he does not curb and control his ambition but allows it to 'run away' with him, he will lose all real joy in life, and, at the last, when it is too late, learn, to his sorrow, that his life, through too much "success," has been a failure.

The writer's experience has been that it is necessary that we should always be progressing, achieving, overcoming and endeavouring to succeed. One of the greatest laws of the Universe is progress, therefore it is fatal to stand still. We must go forward, we must achieve, we must accomplish things. If we do so, we may find that many things which cost us much effort, and hard work are not worth having, yet all the time we are learning, through experience, and are being strengthened and prepared for greater things. Through repeated failure to find true satisfaction, we arrive finally at true knowledge, wisdom and understanding. We are wise then, if, with the world at our feet, we can be satisfied with a very moderate material success, and turn our attention and aspirations to higher and better things.

To win success, either in the hurly-burly of life, or the more difficult path of spiritual progress, demands imagination, vision, courage, faith, determination, persistence, perseverance, hope, cheerfulness and other qualities. These are all to be found within. All these qualities lie more or less dormant within and can be called into expression if we believe that Infinite Power is ours.

.6.

Kahlil Gibran

The Prophet

Lebanese-American poet Kahlil Gibran is best-known for his collection of vivid and striking prose-poetry fables, The Prophet, *which happens to be one of the most translated books in the world. In this excerpt, the Prophet teaches us to strike a harmonious balance between reason and passion, both integral to the creation of a well-rounded life.*

~

On Reason and Passion

And the priestess spoke again and said:
Speak to us of Reason and Passion.
And he answered, saying:
Your soul is oftentimes a battlefield, upon which your
reason and your judgment wage war against
your passion and your appetite.
Would that I could be the peacemaker in your soul, that
I might turn the discord and the rivalry of your elements
into oneness and melody.
But how shall I, unless you yourselves be also the

peacemakers, nay, the lovers of all your elements?
Your reason and your passion are the rudder and the sails of your seafaring soul.
If either your sails or your rudder be broken, you can but toss and drift, or else be held at a standstill in mid-seas. For reason, ruling alone, is a force confining; and passion, unattended, is a flame that burns to its own destruction.
Therefore let your soul exalt your reason to the height of passion, that it may sing;
And let it direct your passion with reason, that your passion may live through its own daily resurrection, and like the phoenix rise above its own ashes.
I would have you consider your judgment and your appetite even as you would two loved guests in your house.
Surely you would not honour one guest above the other; for he who is more mindful of one loses the love and the faith of both
Among the hills, when you sit in the cool shade of the white poplars, sharing the peace and serenity of distant fields and meadows—then let your heart say in silence, "God rests in reason."
And when the storm comes, and the mighty wind shakes the forest, and thunder and lightning proclaim the majesty of the sky,—then let your heart say in awe, "God moves in passion."
And since you are a breath in God's sphere, and a leaf in God's forest, you too should rest in reason and move in passion.

.7.

Arnold Bennett

How to Live on Twenty-four Hours a Day

Of more than two-dozen non-fiction books written by eminent British novelist Arnold Bennett, How to Live on Twenty-four Hours a Day, *has endured ever since its publication in 1908 because of its humorous yet powerful message of hope. In this extract, the author explains how we can discipline our minds to maximize productivity and minimize worry.*

~

People say: 'One can't help one's thoughts.' But one can. The control of the thinking machine is perfectly possible. And since nothing whatever happens to us outside our own brain; since nothing hurts us or gives us pleasure except within the brain, the supreme importance of being able to control what goes on in that mysterious brain is patent. This idea is one of the oldest platitudes, but it is a platitude whose profound truth and urgency most people live and die without realising. People complain of the lack of power to concentrate, not witting that they may acquire the power, if they choose.

And without the power to concentrate—that is to say, without the power to dictate to the brain its task and to ensure obedience—true life is impossible. Mind control is the first element of a full existence.

Hence, it seems to me, the first business of the day should be to put the mind through its paces. You look after your body, inside and out; you run grave danger in hacking hairs off your skin; you employ a whole army of individuals, from the milkman to the pig-killer, to enable you to bribe your stomach into decent behaviour. Why not devote a little attention to the far more delicate machinery of the mind, especially as you will require no extraneous aid? It is for this portion of the art and craft of living that I have reserved the time from the moment of quitting your door to the moment of arriving at your office.

'What? I am to cultivate my mind in the street, on the platform, in the train, and in the crowded street again?' Precisely. Nothing simpler! No tools required! Not even a book. Nevertheless, the affair is not easy.

When you leave your house, concentrate your mind on a subject (no matter what, to begin with). You will not have gone ten yards before your mind has skipped away under your very eyes and is larking round the corner with another subject.

Bring it back by the scruff of the neck. Ere you have reached the station you will have brought it back about forty times. Do not despair. Continue. Keep it up. You will succeed. You cannot by any chance fail if you persevere. It is idle to pretend that your mind is incapable of concentration. Do you not remember that morning when you received a disquieting letter which demanded a very carefully-worded answer? How you kept your mind steadily on the subject of the answer, without a second's intermission, until you reached your office; whereupon you instantly sat down and wrote the answer? That was a case in which *you* were roused by circumstances to such a degree of vitality that you were able to dominate your mind like a tyrant. You would have no trifling. You insisted that its work should be done, and its work was done.

By the regular practice of concentration (as to which there is no secret—save the secret of perseverance) you can tyrannize over your mind (which is not the highest part of *you*) every hour of the day, and in no matter what place. The exercise is a very convenient one. If you got into your morning train with a pair of dumb-bells for your muscles or an encyclopaedia in ten volumes for your learning, you would probably excite remark. But as you walk in the street, or sit in the corner of the compartment behind a pipe, or 'strap-hang' on the Subterranean, who is to know that you are engaged in the most important of daily acts? What asinine boor can laugh at you?

I do not care what you concentrate on, so long as you concentrate. It is the mere disciplining of the thinking machine that counts. But still, you may as well kill two birds with one stone, and concentrate on something useful. I suggest—it is only a suggestion—a little chapter of Marcus Aurelius or Epictetus.

Do not, I beg, shy at their names. For myself, I know nothing more 'actual', more bursting with plain commonsense, applicable to the daily life of plain persons like you and me (who hate airs, pose, and nonsense) than Marcus Aurelius or Epictetus. Read a chapter—and so short they are, the chapters!—in the evening and concentrate on it the next morning. You will see.

Yes, my friend, it is useless for you to try to disguise the fact. I can hear your brain like a telephone at my ear. You are saying to yourself: 'This fellow was doing pretty well up to his seventh chapter. He had begun to interest me faintly. But what he says about thinking in trains, and concentration, and so on, is not for me. It may be well enough for some folks, but it isn't in my line.'

It is for you, I passionately repeat; it is for you. Indeed, you are the very man I am aiming at.

Throw away the suggestion, and you throw away the most precious suggestion that was ever offered to you. It is not my suggestion. It is the suggestion of the most sensible, practical, hard-headed men who have walked the earth. I only give it to you second-hand. Try it. Get your mind in hand. And see how the process cures half the evils of life—especially worry, that miserable, avoidable, shameful disease—worry!

SECTION II

GETTING THE BEST OUT OF YOURSELF

.8.

Joseph Murphy

The Power of Your Subconscious Mind

Joseph Murphy was an Irish author who spent a significant amount of time in India studying Hindu philosophy. His most famous book, The Power of Your Subconscious Mind, *has been a perennial bestseller across the world. In this extract, he tells us how to discipline our subconscious mind to achieve desired results.*

~

You have a mind, and you should learn how to use it. There are two levels of your mind—the conscious or rational level, and the subconscious or irrational level. You think with your conscious mind, and whatever you habitually think sinks down into your subconscious mind, which creates according to the nature of your thoughts. Your subconscious mind is the seat of your emotions and is the creative mind. If you think good, good will follow; if you think evil, evil will follow. This is the way your mind works.

The main point to remember is once the subconscious mind accepts an idea, it begins to execute it. It is an interesting and subtle truth that the law of the subconscious mind works for good and bad ideas alike. This law, when applied in a negative way, is the cause of failure, frustration, and unhappiness. However, when your habitual thinking is harmonious and constructive, you experience perfect health, success, and prosperity.

Peace of mind and a healthy body are inevitable when you begin to think and feel in the right way. Whatever you claim mentally and feel as true, your subconscious mind will accept and bring forth into your experience. The only thing necessary for you to do is to get your subconscious mind to accept your idea, and the law of your own subconscious mind will bring forth the health, peace, or the position you desire. You give the command or decree, and your subconscious will faithfully reproduce the idea impressed upon it. The law of your mind is this: You will get a reaction or response from your subconscious mind according to the nature of the thought or idea you hold in your conscious mind.

Psychologists and psychiatrists point out that when thoughts are conveyed to your subconscious mind, impressions are made in the brain cells. As soon as your subconscious accepts any idea, it proceeds to put it into effect immediately. It works by association of ideas and uses every bit of knowledge that you have gathered in your lifetime to bring about its purpose. It draws on the infinite power, energy, and wisdom within you. It lines up all the laws of nature to get its way. Sometimes it seems to bring about an immediate solution to your difficulties, but at other times it may take days, weeks, or longer. . . . *Its ways are past finding out.*

You must remember that conscious and subconscious minds are not two minds. They are merely two spheres of activity within one mind. Your conscious mind is the reasoning mind. It is that phase of mind, which chooses. For example, you choose your books, your home, and your partner in life. You make all your decisions with your conscious mind. On the other hand, without any conscious choice on your part, your heart is kept functioning automatically, and the process of digestion, circulation, and breathing is carried on by your subconscious mind through processes independent of your conscious control.

Your subconscious mind accepts what is impressed upon it or what you consciously believe. It does not reason things out like your conscious mind, and it does not argue with you controversially. Your subconscious mind is like the soil, which accepts any kind of seed, good or bad. Your thoughts are active and might be likened unto seeds. Negative, destructive thoughts continue to work negatively in your subconscious mind, and in due time will come forth into outer experience, which corresponds with them.

Remember, your subconscious mind does not engage in proving whether your thoughts are good or bad, true or false, but it responds according to the nature of your thoughts or suggestions. For example, if you consciously assume something as true, even though it may be false, your subconscious mind will accept it as true and proceed to bring about results, which must necessarily follow, because you consciously assumed it to be true.

.9.

Orison Swett Marden

Cheerfulness as a Life Power

American author and founder of Success *magazine, Orison Swett Marden's prolific writings on triumph in the face of adversity have inspired millions, including stalwarts like Theodore Roosevelt and Henry Ford. In this excerpt entitled 'The Sunshine Man', the author shows that nurturing a profound sense of hope and gratitude has a domino effect, uplifting both our souls and the world around us.*

~

'There's the dearest little old gentleman,' says James Buckham, 'who goes into town every morning on the 8.30 train. I don't know his name, and yet I know him better than anybody else in town. He just radiates cheerfulness as far as you can see him. There is always a smile on his face, and I never heard him open his mouth except to say something kind, courteous, or good-natured. Everybody bows to him, even strangers, and he bows to everybody, yet never with the slightest hint of presumption or familiarity. If the weather is fine, his jolly compliments make it seem finer; and if it is raining, the merry way in which he speaks of it is as good as a rainbow. Everybody who goes in on the 8.30 train knows the sunshine-man; it's his train. You just hurry up a little, and I'll show you the sunshine-man this morning. It's foggy and cold, but if one look at him doesn't cheer you up so that you'll want to whistle, then I'm no judge of human nature.'

'Good morning, Sir!' said Mr. Jolliboy in going to the same train.

'Why, Sir, I don't know you,' replied Mr. Neversmile.

'I didn't say you did, Sir. Good morning, Sir!'

'The inborn geniality of some people,' says Whipple, 'amounts to genius.'

'How in our troubled lives,' asks J. Freeman Clarke, 'could we do without these fair, sunny natures, into which on their creation-day God allowed nothing sour, acrid, or bitter to enter, but made them a perpetual solace and comfort by their cheerfulness?'

There are those whose very presence carries sunshine with them wherever they go; a sunshine which means pity for the poor, sympathy for the suffering, help for the unfortunate, and benignity toward all. Everybody loves the sunny soul. His very face is a passport anywhere. All doors fly open to him. He disarms prejudice and envy, for he bears good will to everybody. He is as welcome in every household as the sunshine.

'He was quiet, cheerful, genial,' says Carlyle in his *Reminiscences*, concerning Edward Irving's sunny helpfulness. 'His soul unruffled, clear as a mirror, honestly loving and loved, Irving's voice was to me one of blessedness and new hope.'

And to William Wilberforce the poet Southey paid this tribute: 'I never saw any other man who seemed to enjoy such perpetual serenity and sunshine of spirit.'

'I resolved,' said Tom Hood, 'that, like the sun, so long as my day lasted, I would look on the bright side of everything.'

When Goldsmith was in Flanders he discovered the happiest man he had ever seen. At his toil, from morning till night, he was full of song and laughter. Yet this sunny-hearted being was a slave, maimed, deformed, and wearing a chain. How well he illustrated that saying which bids us, if there is no bright side, to polish up the dark one! "Mirth is like the flash of lightning that breaks through the gloom of the clouds and glitters for a moment; cheerfulness keeps up a daylight in the soul, filling it with a steady and perpetual serenity." It is cheerfulness that has the staying quality, like the sunshine changing a world of gloom into a paradise of beauty.

The first prize at a flower-show was taken by a pale, sickly little girl, who lived in a close, dark court in the east of London. The judges asked how she could grow it in such a dingy and sunless place. She replied that a little ray of sunlight came into the court; as soon as it appeared in the morning, she put her flower beneath it, and, as it moved, moved the flower, so that she kept it in the sunlight all day.

'Water, air, and sunshine, the three greatest hygienic agents, are free, and within the reach of all. Twelve years ago,' says Walt Whitman, 'I came to Camden to die. But every day I went into the country, and bathed in the sunshine, lived with the birds and squirrels, and played in the water with the fishes. I received my health from Nature.'

'It is the unqualified result of all my experience with the sick,' said Florence Nightingale, 'that second only to their need of fresh air, is their need of light; that, after a close room, what most hurts them is a dark room; and that it is not only light but direct sunshine they want.'

'Sunlight,' says Dr L. W. Curtis, 'has much to do in keeping air in a healthy condition. No plant can grow in the dark, neither can man remain healthy in a dark, ill-ventilated room. When the first asylum for the blind was erected in Massachusetts, the committee decided to save expenses by not having any windows. They reasoned that, as the patients could not see, there was no need for any light. It was built without windows, but the ventilation was well provided for, and the poor sightless patients were domiciled in the house. But things did not go well: one after another began to sicken, and great languor fell upon them; they felt distressed and restless, craving something, they hardly knew what. After two had died and all were ill, the committee decided to have windows. The sunlight poured in, and the white faces recovered their colour; their flagging energies and depressed spirits revived, and health was restored.'

The sun, making all living things grow, exerts its happiest influence in cheering the mind of man and making his heart glad, and if a man has sunshine in his soul he will go on his way rejoicing; content to look forward if under a cloud, not bating one jot of heart or hope if for a moment cast down; honouring his occupation, whatever it be; rendering even rags respectable by the way he wears them; and not only happy himself but giving happiness to others.

How a man's face shines when illuminated by a great moral motive! and his manner, too, is touched with the grace of light.

'Nothing will supply the want of sunshine to peaches,' said Emerson, 'and to make knowledge valuable you must have the cheerfulness of wisdom.'

'Wondrous is the strength of cheerfulness,' said Carlyle, 'altogether past calculation its powers of endurance. Efforts to be permanently useful must be uniformly joyous—a spirit all sunshine, graceful from very gladness, beautiful because bright.'

'The cheerful man carries with him perpetually, in his presence and personality, an influence that acts upon others as summer warmth on the fields and forests. It wakes up and calls out the best that is in them. It makes them stronger, braver, and happier. Such a man makes a little spot of this world a lighter, brighter, warmer place for other people to live in. To meet him in the morning is to get inspiration which makes all the day's struggles and tasks easier. His hearty handshake puts a thrill of new vigour into your veins. After talking with him for a few minutes, you feel an exhilaration of spirits, a quickening of energy, a renewal of zest and interest in living, and are ready for any duty or service.'

'Great hearts there are among men,' says Hillis, of Plymouth pulpit, 'they carry a volume of manhood; their presence is sunshine; their coming changes our climate; they oil the bearings of life; their shadow always falls behind them; they make right living easy. Blessed are the happiness-makers: they represent the best forces in civilization!'

If refined manners reprove us a little for ill-timed laughter, a smiling face kindled by a smiling heart is always in order. Who can ever forget Emerson's smile? It was a perpetual benediction upon all who knew him. A smile is said to be to the human countenance what sunshine is to the landscape. Or a smile is called the rainbow of the face.

'This is a dark world to many people,' says a suggestive modern writer, 'a world of chills, a world of fogs, a world of wet blankets. Nine-tenths of the men we meet need encouragement. Your work is so urgent that you have no time to stop and speak to the people, but every day you meet scores, perhaps hundreds and thousands of persons, upon whom you might have direct and immediate influence. "How? How?" you cry out. We answer: by the grace of physiognomy. There is nothing more catching than a face with a lantern behind it, shining clear through. We have no admiration for a face with a dry smile, meaning no more than the grin of a false face. But a smile written by the hand of God, as an index finger or table of contents, to whole volumes of good feeling within, is a benediction. You say: "My face is hard and lacking in mobility, and my benignant feelings are not observable in the facial proportions." We do not believe you. Freshness and geniality of the soul are so subtle and pervading that they will, at some eye or mouth corner, leak out. Set behind your face a feeling of gratitude to God and kindliness toward man, and you will every day preach a sermon long as the streets you walk, a sermon with as many heads as the number of people you meet, and differing from other sermons in the fact that the longer it is the better. The reason that there are so many sour faces, so many frowning faces, so many dull faces, is because men consent to be acrid and petulant, and stupid. The way to improve your face is to improve your disposition. Attractiveness of physiognomy does not depend on regularity of features. We know persons whose brows are shaggy, eyes oblique, noses ominously longitudinal, and mouths straggling along in unusual and unexpected directions; and yet they are men and women of so much soul that we love to look upon them, and their faces are sweet evangels.'

It was N. P. Willis, I think, who added to the beatitudes: 'Blessed are the joy-makers. And this is why all the world loves little children, who are always ready to have "a sunshine party"—little children bubbling over with fun, as a bobolink with song. How well we remember it all!—the long gone years of our own childhood, and the households of joyous children we have known in later years. Joy-makers are the children still—some of them in unending scenes of light. I saw but yesterday this epitaph at Mount Auburn—*she was so pleasant: sunny-hearted in life, and now alive forever more in light supernal.*'

'How can we then but rejoice with joy unspeakable, as the children of immortality; living habitually above the gloom and damps of earth, and leading lives of ministration; bestowing everywhere sweetness and light—radiating upon the earth something of the beauty of the unseen world.'

What is a sunny temper but 'a talisman more powerful

than wealth, more precious than rubies'? What is it but 'an aroma whose fragrance fills the air with the odours of Paradise'?

'I am so full of happiness,' said a little child, 'that I could not be any happier unless I could grow.' And she bade "good morning" to her sweet singing bird, and "good morning" to the sun; then she asked her mother's permission, and softly, reverently, gladly bade "good morning to God"—and why should she not?'

Was it not Goethe who represented a journey that followed the sunshine round the world, forever bathed in light? And Longfellow sang:

It is always morning somewhere; and above
The awakening continents, from shore to shore,
Somewhere the birds are singing evermore.

The darkness past, we mount the radiant skies,
And changeless day is ours; we hear the songs
Of higher spheres, the light divine our eyes
Behold and sunlight robes of countless throngs
Who dwell in light; we seek, with joyous quest,
God's service sweet to wipe all tears away,
And list we every hour, with eager zest,
For high command to toils that God has blest:
So fill we full our endless sunshine day.

.10.

Kahlil Gibran

The Prophet

In this poetic essay, Kahlil Gibran addresses a deeply universal concern: how to navigate both joy and sorrow without succumbing to extremities. Here, the Prophet tells us to experience the richness of human emotions, that joy and grief are inseparable, and it is not possible to experience one without the other.

~

On Joy and Sorrow

Then a woman said, Speak to us of Joy and Sorrow.
And he answered:
Your joy is your sorrow unmasked.
And the selfsame well from which your laughter rises was oftentimes filled with your tears.
And how else can it be?
The deeper that sorrow carves into your being, the more joy you can contain.
Is not the cup that holds your wine the very cup that was burned in the potter's oven?

And is not the lute that soothes your spirit, the very
wood that was hollowed with knives?
When you are joyous, look deep into your heart and you
shall find it is only that which has given you sorrow that
is giving you joy.
When you are sorrowful look again in your heart, and
you shall see that in truth you are weeping for that
which has been your delight.
Some of you say, "Joy is greater than sorrow," and others
say, "Nay, sorrow is the greater."
But I say unto you, they are inseparable.
Together they come, and when one sits alone with
you at your board, remember that the other is asleep
upon your bed.

Verily you are suspended like scales between your
sorrow and your joy.
Only when you are empty are you at standstill and
balanced.
When the treasure-keeper lifts you to weigh his gold and
his silver, needs must your joy or your sorrow rise or
fall.

.11.

James Allen

Above Life's Turmoil

In this extract entitled 'Sowing and Reaping', the author proves how well-directed thoughts rooted in compassion and service will always yield happiness and victory. However, words and deeds arising from selfishness only beget more selfishness.

~

Go into the fields and country lanes in the spring-time, and you will see farmers and gardeners busy sowing seeds in the newly prepared soil. If you were to ask any one of those gardeners or farmers what kind of produce he expected from the seed he was sowing, he would doubtless regard you as foolish, and would tell you that he does not 'expect' at all, that it is a matter of common knowledge that his produce will be of the kind which he is sowing and that he is sowing wheat, or barley, or turnips, as the case may be, in order to reproduce that particular kind.

Every fact and process in Nature contains a moral lesson for the wise man. There is no law in the world of Nature around us which is not to be found operating with the same mathematical certainty in the mind of man and in human life. All the parables of Jesus are illustrative of this truth and are drawn from the simple facts of Nature. There is a process of seed-sowing in the mind and life a spiritual sowing which leads to a harvest according to the kind of seed sown. Thoughts, words, and acts are seeds sown, and, by the inviolable law of things, they produce after their kind.

The man who thinks hateful thoughts brings hatred upon himself. The man who thinks loving thoughts is loved. The man whose thoughts, words and acts are sincere, is surrounded by sincere friends; the insincere man is surrounded by insincere friends. The man who sows wrong thoughts and deeds, and prays that God will bless him, is in the position of a farmer who, having sown tares, asks God to bring forth for him a harvest of wheat.

> *"That which ye sow, ye reap; see yonder fields*
> *The sesamum was sesamum, the corn*
> *Was corn; the silence and the darkness knew;*
> *So is a man's fate born."*
> *"He cometh reaper of the things he sowed."*

He who would be blest, let him scatter blessings. He who would be happy, let him consider the happiness of others.

Then there is another side to this seed sowing. The farmer must scatter all his seed upon the land, and then leave it to the elements. Were he to covetously hoard his seed, he would lose both it and his produce, for his seed would perish. It perishes when he sows it, but in perishing it brings forth a great abundance. So in life, we get by giving; we grow rich by scattering. The man who says he is in possession of knowledge which he cannot give out because the world is incapable of receiving it, either does not possess such knowledge, or, if he does, will soon be deprived of it - if he is not already so deprived. To hoard is to lose; to exclusively retain is to be dispossessed.

Even the man who would increase his material wealth must be willing to part with (invest) what little capital he has, and then wait for the increase. So long as he retains his hold on his precious money, he will not only remain poor, but will be growing poorer every day. He will, after all, lose the thing he loves, and will lose it without increase. But if he wisely lets it go; if, like the farmer, he scatters his seeds of gold, then he can faithfully wait for, and reasonably expect, the increase.

Men are asking God to give them peace and purity, and righteousness and blessedness, but are not obtaining these things; and why not? Because they are not practising them, not sowing them. I once heard a preacher pray very earnestly for forgiveness, and shortly afterwards, in the course of his sermon, he called upon his congregation to 'show no mercy to the enemies of the church'. Such self-delusion is pitiful, and men have yet to learn that the way to obtain peace and blessedness is to scatter peaceful and blessed thoughts, words, and deeds.

Men believe that they can sow the seeds of strife, impurity, and unbrotherliness, and then gather in a rich harvest of peace, purity and concord by merely asking for it. What more pathetic sight than to see an irritable and quarrelsome man praying for peace. Men reap that which they sow, and any man can reap all blessedness now and at once, if he will put aside selfishness, and sow broadcast the seeds of kindness, gentleness, and love.

If a man is troubled, perplexed, sorrowful, or unhappy, let him ask:

'What mental seeds have I been sowing?'

'What seeds am I sowing?'

'What have I done for others?'

'What is my attitude towards others?'

'What seeds of trouble and sorrow and unhappiness have I sown that I should thus reap these bitter weeds?'

Let him seek within and find, and having found, let him abandon all the seeds of self, and sow, henceforth, only the seeds of Truth.

Let him learn of the farmer the simple truths of wisdom.

.12.

Neema Majumdar, Nandini Mirani, and Saloni Jhaveri

Finding Meaning in Life with the Bhagavad Gita

In Verse 30, Lord Krishna illuminates the route to self-growth through a framework involving three attributes (gunas) of the mind: sattva, rajas, and tamas.

~

The Sattva—Rajas—Tamas Framework

सत्वं रजस्तम इति गुणाः प्रकृतिसम्भवाः ।
निबध्नन्ति महाबाहो देहे देहिनमव्ययम् ॥14-5॥

*sattvaṁ rajastama iti guṇāḥ prakṛtisambhavāḥ
nibadhnanti mahābāho dehe dehinam avyayam*

Arjuna, the mighty armed! Sattva, rajas, and tamas, the qualities existing in prakriti, bind (as though) the changeless indweller of the body, to the body. (14.5)

~

The mind with its attributes is itself an object, like every other object in the universe.

Sattva represents such qualities as purity, harmony, truthfulness, accommodation, and compassion. A person who has primarily these qualities is called a sattvika person.

Rajas indicates an action-based outlook but can also include an overriding self-interest and personal ambition, greed, pride, or arrogance. Such a person is rajasika.

Tamas is being mostly lazy, indolent, fearful, confused, disinterested, or led by the senses. This would make a person tamasika.

We have a tendency to consider a person sattvika, rajasika, or tamasika based on what they do—a scientist is considered to be sattvika because of his profession. However, it is not the profession which demonstrates the guna—rather, it is the underlying attitude and intention. If the scientist is motivated by a quest for knowledge and to help humanity, then he is sattvika. If he is driven by a search for awards and personal recognition, he is rajasika. If he has a disposition to skew data for showing convenient results, then he is tamasika.

Everyone, from an assembly line worker to the head of an organization is sattvika, if they execute their role with dedication, sincerity, and keeping the welfare of the company in mind. Similarly, acts of giving (danam) as well as acts of austerity and self-discipline (tapas) appear to be sattvik. However, if under the pretext of giving we want to take advantage of others, then the act is tamasik. If fasting is only for the sake of vanity, then it is rajasik.

To become sattvika is multidimensional and involves deliberate effort and action in all areas of our life. Even becoming sattvika is a means to an end and not an end in itself. We have to use our sattvik mind to dispel our confusion about the nature of 'I'.

.13.

Arnold Bennett

How to Live on Twenty-four Hours a Day

In this section entitled 'Dangers to Avoid', the author warns us against the often-ignored, but extremely damaging, pitfalls commonly encountered in the winding path to self-discovery and how we can choose to overcome them and tap into our inner desires.

~

I cannot terminate these hints, often, I fear, too didactic and abrupt, upon the full use of one's time to the great end of living (as distinguished from vegetating) without briefly referring to certain dangers which lie in wait for the sincere aspirant towards life. The first is the terrible danger of becoming that most odious and least supportable of persons—a prig. Now a prig is a pert fellow who gives himself airs of superior wisdom. A prig is a pompous fool who has gone out for a ceremonial walk, and without knowing it has lost an important part of his attire, namely, his sense of humour. A prig is a tedious individual who, having made a discovery, is so impressed by his discovery that he is capable of being gravely displeased because the entire world is not also impressed by it. Unconsciously to become a prig is an easy and a fatal thing.

Hence, when one sets forth on the enterprise of using all one's time, it is just as well to remember that one's own time, and not other people's time, is the material with which one has to deal; that the earth rolled on pretty comfortably before one began to balance a budget of the hours, and that it will continue to roll on pretty comfortably whether or not one succeeds in one's new role of chancellor of the exchequer of time. It is as well not to chatter too much about what one is doing, and not to betray a too-pained sadness at the spectacle of a whole world deliberately wasting so many hours out of every day, and therefore never really living. It will be found, ultimately, that in taking care of one's self one has quite all one can do.

Another danger is the danger of being tied to a programme like a slave to a chariot. One's programme must not be allowed to run away with one. It must be respected, but it must not be worshipped as a fetish. A programme of daily employ is not a religion.

This seems obvious. Yet I know men whose lives are a burden to themselves and a distressing burden to their relatives and friends simply because they have failed to appreciate the obvious. "Oh, no," I have heard the martyred wife exclaim, "Arthur always takes the dog out for exercise at eight o'clock and he always begins to read at a quarter to nine. So it's quite out of the question that we should…" etc., etc. And the note of absolute finality in that plaintive voice reveals the unsuspected and ridiculous tragedy of a career.

On the other hand, a programme is a programme. And

unless it is treated with deference it ceases to be anything but a poor joke. To treat one's programme with exactly the right amount of deference, to live with not too much and not too little elasticity, is scarcely the simple affair it may appear to the inexperienced.

And still, another danger is the danger of developing a policy of rush, of being gradually more and more obsessed with what one has to do next. In this way, one may come to exist as in a prison, and one's life may cease to be one's own. One may take the dog out for a walk at eight o'clock, and meditate the whole time on the fact that one must begin to read at a quarter to nine, and that one must not be late.

And the occasional deliberate breaking of one's programme will not help to mend matters. The evil springs not from persisting without elasticity in what one has attempted, but from originally attempting too much, from filling one's programme till it runs over. The only cure is to reconstitute the programme and to attempt less.

But the appetite for knowledge grows by what it feeds on, and there are men who come to like a constant breathless hurry of endeavour. Of them, it may be said that a constant breathless hurry is better than an eternal doze.

In any case, if the programme exhibits a tendency to be oppressive, and yet one wishes not to modify it, an excellent palliative is to pass with exaggerated deliberation from one portion of it to another; for example, to spend five minutes in perfect mental quiescence between chaining up the St. Bernard and opening the book; in other words, to waste five minutes with the entire consciousness of wasting them.

The last, and chiefest danger which I would indicate, is one to which I have already referred—the risk of a failure at the commencement of the enterprise.

I must insist on it.

A failure at the commencement may easily kill outright the newborn impulse towards a complete vitality, and therefore every precaution should be observed to avoid it. The impulse must not be over-taxed. Let the pace of the first lap be even absurdly slow, but let it be as regular as possible.

And, having once decided to achieve a certain task, achieve it at all costs of tedium and distaste. The gain in self-confidence of having accomplished a tiresome labour is immense.

Finally, in choosing the first occupations of those evening hours, be guided by nothing whatever but your taste and natural inclination.

It is a fine thing to be a walking encyclopaedia of philosophy, but if you happen to have no liking for philosophy, and to have a like for the natural history of street-cries, much better leave philosophy alone, and take to street-cries.

.14.

Arthur Schopenhauer

Counsels and Maxims

One of the most influential German philosophers of the eighteenth century, Arthur Schopenhauer's philosophies have influenced the likes of Albert Einstein, Sigmund Freud, Leo Tolstoy, and Herman Hesse. In this tract, he stresses on the need to appreciate life in its entirety, glean insights from its experiences, and evade fixating on objects that only provide short-lived happiness.

~

Care should be taken not to build the happiness of life

...upon a broad foundation—not to require a great many things in order to be happy. For happiness on such a foundation is the most easily undermined; it offers many more opportunities for accidents; and accidents are always happening. The architecture of happiness follows a plan in this respect just the opposite of that adopted in every other case, where the broadest foundation offers the greatest security. Accordingly, to reduce your claims to the lowest possible degree, in comparison with your mean—of whatever kind these may be—is the surest way of avoiding extreme misfortune.

To make extensive preparations for life—no matter what form they may take—is one of the greatest and commonest of follies. Such preparations presuppose, in the first place, a long life, the full and complete term of years appointed to man—and how few reach it! And even if it be reached, it is still too short for all the plans that have been made; for to carry them out requites more time than was thought necessary at the beginning. And then how many mischances and obstacles stand in the way! how seldom the goal is ever reached in human affairs!

And lastly, even though the goal should be reached, the changes which Time works in us have been left out of the reckoning: we forget that the capacity whether for achievement or for enjoyment does not last a whole lifetime. So we often toil for things which are no longer suited to us when we attain them; and again, the years we spend preparing for some work, unconsciously rob us of the power for carrying it out.

How often it happens that a man is unable to enjoy the wealth which he acquired at so much trouble and risk, and that the fruits of his labour are reserved for others; or that he is incapable of filling the position which he has won after so many years of toil and struggle. Fortune has come too late for him; or, contrarily, he has come too late for fortune—when, for instance, he wants to achieve great things, say, in art or literature: the popular taste has changed, it may be; a new generation has grown up, which takes no interest in his work; others have gone a shorter way and got the start of him. These are the facts of life which Horace must have had in view when he lamented the uselessness of all advice—

> *Quid eternis minorem*
> *Consiliis animum fatigas?**

The cause of this commonest of all follies is that optical illusion of the mind from which everyone suffers, making life, at its beginning, seem of long duration; and at its end, when one looks back over the course of it, how short a time it seems! There is some advantage in the illusion; but for it, no great work would ever be done.

Our life is like a journey on which, as we advance, the landscape takes a different view from that which it presented at first, and changes again, as we come nearer. This is just what happens—especially with our wishes. We often find something else, nay, something better than what we are looking for; and what we look for, we often find on a very different path from that on which we began a vain search. Instead of finding, as we expected, pleasure, happiness, joy, we get experience, insight, knowledge—a real and permanent blessing, instead of a fleeting and illusory one.

This is the thought that runs through *Wilhelm Meister*, like the bass in a piece of music. In this work of Goethe's, we

---

*No flowers in constant form remain,
the Moons with changing horn revolve,
nor can the mind's exhausted strain,
the problem of 'forever' solve.
From *The Odes of Horace*, translated by W. E. Gladstone.

have a novel of the intellectual kind, and, therefore, superior to all others, even to Sir Walter Scott's, which are, one and all, ethical; in other words, they treat of human nature only from the side of the will. So, too, in the *Zauberflöte*—that grotesque, but still significant, and even hieroglyphic—the same thought is symbolized, but in great, coarse lines, much in the way in which scenery is painted. Here the symbol would be complete if Tamino were in the end to be cured of his desire to possess Tainina, and received, in her stead, initiation into the mysteries of the Temple of Wisdom. It is quite right for Papageno, his necessary contrast, to succeed in getting his Papagena.

Men of any worth or value soon come to see that they are in the hands of Fate, and gratefully submit to be moulded by its teachings. They recognize that the fruit of life is experience, and not happiness; they become accustomed and content to exchange hope for insight; and, in the end, they can say, with Petrarch, that all they care for is to learn—

Altro diletto che 'mparar, non provo*.

It may even be that they to some extent still follow their old wishes and aims, trifling with them, as it were, for the sake of appearances; all the while really and seriously looking for nothing but instruction; a process which lends them an air of genius, a trait of something contemplative and sublime.

In their search for gold, the alchemists discovered other things—gunpowder, china, medicines, the laws of nature. There is a sense in which we are all alchemists.

---

*The greatest pleasure lies in learning.

SECTION III
FINDING INNER STRENGTH

.15.

Napoleon Hill

Think and Grow Rich

In this section entitled 'Three Feet from Gold', Napoleon Hill reveals how failure rears its ugly head when we are closest to success, and in such a scenario, it is only the act of persevering that will bridge the gap between where we are and where we want to be.

~

One of the most common causes of failure is the habit of quitting when one is overtaken by temporary defeat. Every person is guilty of this mistake at one time or another. An uncle of R. U. Darby was caught by the 'gold fever' in the goldrush days and went west to DIG AND GROW RICH. He had never heard that more gold has been mined from the brains of men than has ever been taken from the earth. He staked a claim and went to work with pick and shovel. The going was hard, but his lust for gold was definite.

After weeks of labour, he was rewarded by the discovery of the shining ore. He needed machinery to bring the ore to the surface. Quietly, he covered up the mine, retraced his footsteps to his home in Williamsburg, Maryland, told his relatives and a few neighbours of the 'strike'. They got together the money for the needed machinery, had it shipped. The uncle and Darby went back to work the mine. The first car of ore was mined, and shipped to a smelter. The returns proved they had one of the richest mines in Colorado! A few more cars of that ore would clear the debts. Then would come the big killing in profits.

Down went the drills! Up went the hopes of Darby and Uncle! Then something happened! The vein of gold ore disappeared! They had come to the end of the rainbow, and the pot of gold was no longer there! They drilled on, desperately trying to pick up the vein again-all to no avail.

Finally, they decided to QUIT. They sold the machinery to a junk man for a few hundred dollars and took the train back home. Some 'junk' men are dumb, but not this one! He called in a mining engineer to look at the mine and do a little calculating. The engineer advised that the project had failed because the owners were not familiar with "fault lines." His calculations showed that the vein would be found JUST THREE FEET FROM WHERE THE DARBYS HAD STOPPED DRILLING! That is exactly where it was found!

The 'Junk' man took millions of dollars in ore from the mine because he knew enough to seek expert counsel before giving up. Most of the money which went into the machinery was procured through the efforts of R. U. Darby, who was then a very young man. The money came from his relatives and neighbours, because of their faith in him. He paid back every dollar of it, although he was years in doing so.

Long afterwards, Mr. Darby recouped his loss many times over, when he made the discovery that DESIRE can be transmuted into gold. The discovery came after he went into the business of selling life insurance. Remembering that he lost a huge fortune because he STOPPED three feet from gold, Darby profited from the experience in his chosen work, by the simple method of saying to himself, 'I stopped three feet from gold, but I will never stop because men say `no' when I ask them to buy insurance.'

Darby is one of a small group of fewer than fifty men who sell more than a million dollars in life insurance annually. He owes his 'stickability' to the lesson he learned from his 'quitability' in the gold mining business.

Before success comes in any man's life, he is sure to meet with much temporary defeat, and, perhaps, some failure. When defeat overtakes a man, the easiest and most logical thing to do is to QUIT. That is exactly what the majority of men do. More than five hundred of the most successful men this country has ever known told the author their greatest success came just one step beyond the point at which defeat had overtaken them. Failure is a trickster with a keen sense of irony and cunning. It takes great delight in tripping one when success is almost within reach.

.16.

Neema Majumdar, Nandini Mirani, and Saloni Jhaveri

Finding Meaning in Life with the Bhagavad Gita

Verses 31–32 of the Bhagavad Gita addresses how ego (ahankara), unchecked desire (kama), and anger (krodha) are the most harmful impediments to our personal growth.

~

Obstacles to Growth

अहकारं बलं दर्पं कामं क्रोधं च संश्रिता: ।
मामात्मपरदेहेषु प्रद्विषन्तोऽभ्यसूयका: ॥16-18॥

तानहं द्विषत: क्रूरान्संसारेषु नराधमान् ।
क्षिपाम्यरन्नमशुभानासुरीष्वेव योनिषु ॥16-19॥

*ahaṅkāraṁ balaṁ darpaṁ kāmaṁ krodhaṁ ca saṁśritāḥ
mām ātmaparadeheṣu pradviṣanto'bhyasūyakāḥ*

*tān ahaṁ dviṣataḥ krūrān saàsāreṣu narādhamān
kṣipāmyajasram aśubhān āsurīṣveva yoniṣu*

Those who are completely given to egoism, (brute) strength, insolence, enjoyment, and anger, who despise Me in their own and others' bodies, who are great cavillers

> who are hateful and cruel, who are the lowest of men, who are wrongdoers, I despatch them repeatedly into a life of transmigration only in asuri wombs. (16.18–19)

~

The usual definition of ahankara in Vedanta is the 'I-sense', which is one of the functions of the mind. The mind has an inherent self-reflexive capacity wherein it connects every physiological action of the body and its thoughts to this 'I-sense'. For instance, the signal of hunger sent by the digestive system to the brain is interpreted as 'I am hungry', which is normal and necessary. However, as we live our life, we add our own narratives to our 'I-sense' based on our experiences and our interpretations of them. Sometimes this functional 'I' gets inflated and we may develop a sense of superiority based on our intellect or wealth. This is commonly termed 'ego'.

Kama refers to desire. Human beings are born with the privileged abilities to desire (iccha shakti), to know (jnana shakti) and to do (kriya shakti). Desires become a liability only when we lose perspective in their pursuit. For example, though a desire for wealth is not inherently harmful, it is distorted if it leads us to cheat others. When desire comes into conflict with dharma and we succumb, then it is unhealthy. Desires change through life—they are age and stage specific. Our desire for toys when we were children can move to college admissions, marriage, promotions, and legacy as we grow older. In pursuing each of these, we can lose perspective.

Krodha refers to anger. Life is a journey and is designed in a way that we experience both pleasure and pain. Different situations evoke different emotions. Unresolved pain can be a source of anger leading to aggression, or can remain passive and emerge as depression over time.

If we do not correct these shortcomings, we live with an unhealthy 'I-sense', unchecked desire, and overwhelming emotion. Actions that stem from this confused mindset cause suffering to ourselves and others. When left unaddressed, the consequences get magnified, taking us into a downward spiral. We remain entangled, multiplying our sufferings in the present and future.

.17.

Joseph Murphy

The Power of Your Subconscious Mind

In this section, the author talks about how every individual must make a conscious and deliberate effort to desire and 'choose' joy every step of the way, so that being happy becomes a virtuous habit that one can never shake off.

~

You Must Choose Happiness

Happiness is a state of mind. There is a phrase in the Bible which says, 'Choose ye this day whom ye will serve. You have the freedom to choose happiness.' This may seem extraordinarily simple, and it is. Perhaps this is why people stumble over the way to happiness; they do not see the simplicity of the key to happiness. The great things in life are simple, dynamic, and creative. They produce well-being and happiness.

How to Choose Happiness?

Begin now to choose happiness. This is how you do it: when you open your eyes in the morning, say to yourself, 'Divine order takes charge of my life today and every day. All things work together for good for me today. This is a new and wonderful day for me. There will never be another day like this one. I am divinely guided all day long, and whatever I do will prosper. Divine love surrounds me, enfolds me, and enwraps me, and I go forth in peace. Whenever my attention wanders away from that which is good and constructive, I will immediately bring it back to the contemplation of that which is lovely and of good report. I am a spiritual and mental magnet attracting to myself all things, which bless and prosper me. I am going to be a wonderful success in all my undertakings today. I am definitely going to be happy all day long.'

Start each day in this manner; then you will be choosing happiness, and you will be a radiant joyous person.

He Made It a Habit to Be Happy

A number of years ago, I stayed for about a week in a farmer's house in Connemarra on the west coast of Ireland. He seemed to be always singing and whistling and was full of humour. I asked him the secret of his happiness, and his reply was: 'It is a habit of mine to be happy. Every morning when I awaken and every night before I go to sleep, I bless my family, the crops, the cattle, and I thank God for the wonderful harvest.' This farmer had made a practice of this for over forty years. As you know, thoughts repeated regularly and systematically sink into the subconscious mind and become habitual. He discovered that happiness is a habit.

You Must Desire to Be Happy

There is one very important point about being happy. You must sincerely desire to be happy. There are people who have been depressed, dejected, and unhappy for so long that was they suddenly made happy by some wonderful, good, joyous news, they would actually be like the woman who said to me, 'It is wrong to be so happy!' They have been so accustomed to the old mental patterns that they do not feel at home being happy! They long for the former, depressed, unhappy state. I knew a woman in England who had rheumatism for many years. She would pat herself on the knee and say, 'My rheumatism is bad today. I cannot go out. My rheumatism keeps me miserable.' This dear elderly lady got a lot of attention from her son, daughter, and the neighbours. She really wanted her rheumatism. She enjoyed her 'misery' as she called it. This woman did not really want to be happy. I suggested a curative procedure to her. I wrote down some biblical verses and told her that if she gave attention to these truths, her mental attitude would undoubtedly change and would result in her faith and confidence in being restored to health. She was not interested. There seems to be a peculiar, mental, morbid streak in many people, whereby they seem to enjoy being miserable and sad.

The Happiest People

The happiest man is he who constantly brings forth and practices what is best in him. Happiness and virtue complement each other. The best are not only the happiest, but the happiest are usually the best in the art of living life successfully. God is the highest and best in you. Express more of God's love, light, truth, and beauty, and you will become one of the happiest persons in the world today. Epictetus, the Greek stoic philosopher, said, 'There is but one way to the tranquillity of mind and happiness; let this, therefore, be always ready at hand with thee, both when thou wakest early in the morning, and all the day long, and when thou goest late to sleep, to account no external things thine own, but commit all these to God.'

.18.

Kahlil Gibran

The Prophet

In this section, the Prophet teaches us that when suppressed emotional hurt comes to the surface, it is a painful experience. However, it is this breakthrough that exposes the wound to sunlight and begins the journey towards happiness and healing.

~

On Pain

And a woman spoke, saying, Tell us of Pain.
And he said:
Your pain is the breaking of the shell that encloses your understanding.
Even as the stone of the fruit must break, that its heart may stand in the sun, so must you know pain.
And could you keep your heart in wonder at the daily miracles of your life, your pain would not seem less wondrous than your joy;
And you would accept the seasons of your heart, even as you have always accepted the seasons that pass over your fields.

And you would watch with serenity through
the winters of your grief.
Much of your pain is self-chosen.
It is the bitter potion by which the physician
within you heals your sick self.
Therefore trust the physician, and drink his remedy in silence and tranquillity: For his hand, though heavy and hard, is guided by the tender hand of the Unseen, And the cup he brings, though it burn your lips, has been fashioned of the clay which the Potter has moistened with His own sacred tears.

.19.

James Allen

How Pain Leads to Knowledge and Power[*]

In this essay, the author gives us a unique perspective on reconciling with the existence of pain in our lives. One must aim to find the root of pain and utilize that knowledge to protect the mind and the body and preserve its integrity.

~

Suffering leads to perfection through successive stages of knowledge—not knowledge from books, but knowledge of life—and each step in knowledge means that some form of suffering has been transmuted and transcended. A particular kind of pain, experienced innumerable times, at last leads to knowledge of the cause of that pain, and when the cause is discovered, removed, and not again entertained, the pain is forever transcended.

This principle is applicable both to physical pain, which is caused by disease, and to mental suffering caused by wrong thinking. When the cause of a disease is known, it can be avoided, and the disease and its pain can never

---

[*]Published in *The Epoch*, a spiritual magazine founded by James Allen.

attack us. The cause of certain forms of disease is known, and the prudent avoid the cause and so escape the disease. The causes of many bodily disorders, however, still await discovery, and until such discovery is affected, the disorders will continue.

In all forms of mental suffering, the cause can be more readily discovered, and when discovered, removed and avoided, because the mind comes more under our immediate control. We cannot eliminate the bodily sensation of pain. The pain caused by direct injury to the body is different from that caused by disease. Thus a perfect man—perfect both in mind and health—would feel pain from a cut or wound, just as a very imperfect man would; and it is necessary for the protection of his body that he should do so, but his bodily pain would be modified by his attitude of mind towards it. It would not cause him any mental suffering and he would retain his happiness and peace of mind. The imperfect man would, however, become disturbed mentally—would be aroused to fear, or agitation, or anger—and so would add mental pain to physical so that even the physical pain would appear greater.

Not one of the Great Teachers has taught men how to overcome bodily pain or annul the bodily sensation of pain. This is highly significant in view of the fact that certain schools of thought aim at this end. This studying and striving to render one's body insensible to pain is no new thing. It was taught and practised in the East thousands of years ago and is known in India as Hatha Yoga, or physical Yoga. If accounts speak truly, there are still Yogis in India who can cut and wound their bodies and not experience pain, and while this is an accomplishment of its kind, it is a bad one and is no indication of spiritual advancement. Indeed this Hatha Yoga was condemned as Black Yoga, or False Yoga by the Great Teachers of India, who declared that it led to bodily disease and spiritual ignorance, and not to health and Truth. The practice taught by the spiritually enlightened was, and is, known as Raja Yoga, meaning kingly Yoga. This kingly or true Yoga consisted in purifying the heart and gaining control of the mind, and the method is embodied in their precepts. The precepts of Jesus outline this practice with great clearness.

It is clear, then, that we should not strive to become insensible to physical pain, first because it is unnatural; and second, because we should thereby deprive ourselves of the warning and protection to our body which such pain affords; but we should endeavour to heal the pain when caused by injury; or find and remove the cause, when it is the result of disease.

Nor should we try to render ourselves insensible to mental pain by any process of hardening. Unnatural as this is, it can be done successfully up to a certain, point, just as insensibility to physical pain can be accomplished to a degree, for as the latter ultimately leads to wreckage of the body, so the former leads to mental disaster, leads one further and further away from Truth, until at last he has to begin all over again.

Nevertheless, mental pain can be transcended, yet not by hardening the heart, but by softening it, by practising oneself in all thoughts and deeds that are good and kind and just, until at last the cause of the mind's suffering is clearly seen and is removed and avoided. Once the cause of any particular kind of mental pain is seen, its elimination from the mind becomes comparatively easy. The thought which originated the deed which produced the pain is gradually reduced in strength, and in the frequency of its recurrence, until it at last disappears entirely from the mind and life. And with each mental pain thus transcended, there is a great advance in knowledge, and it is a divine knowledge which is accompanied by steadfastness, happiness, and power, lifting on able those fluctuations between happiness and misery in which the majority live.

Thus the wise man sees that everything is good, even the presence of pain, and he uses that pain to enable him to reach higher regions of knowledge. Regarding his pain as a sure indication that he has done wrong somewhere, he searches for his mistake, and, having found it, he ever after avoids it.

So in the crucible of pain is the dross of ignorance burnt away from us. Thus are we purified in the fire of knowledge.

.20.

Dale Carnegie

How to Stop Worrying and Start Living

In this excerpt entitled 'What Makes You Tired', the author exposes the root cause of constant fatigue: emotional exhaustion. He provides many valuable tips that can enable us to combat weariness stemming from nervous tension and maximize efficiency in our day-to-day lives.

~

Here is an astounding and significant fact: mental work alone can't make you tired. Sounds absurd. But a few years ago, scientists tried to find out how long the human brain could labour without reaching 'a diminished capacity for work', the scientific definition of fatigue. To the amazement of these scientists, they discovered that blood passing through the brain, when it is active, shows no fatigue at all! If you took blood from the veins of a day labourer while he was working, you would find it full of 'fatigue toxins' and fatigue products. But if you took a drop of blood from the brain of an Albert Einstein, it would show no fatigue toxins whatever at the end of the day.

So far as the brain is concerned, it can work 'as well and as swiftly at the end of eight or even twelve hours of effort as at the beginning'. The brain is utterly tireless.... So what makes you tired? Psychiatrists declare that most of our fatigue derives from our mental and emotional attitudes. One of England's most distinguished psychiatrists, J. A. Hadfield, says in his book, *The Psychology of Power*: 'The greater part of the fatigue from which we suffer is of mental origin; in fact exhaustion of purely physical origin is rare.' One of America's most distinguished psychiatrists, Dr A. A. Brill, goes even further. He declares: 'One hundred per cent of the fatigue of the sedentary worker in good health is due to psychological factors, by which we mean emotional factors.'

What kinds of emotional factors tire the sedentary (or sitting) worker? Joy? Contentment? No! Never! Boredom, resentment, a feeling of not being appreciated, a feeling of futility, hurry, anxiety, worry those are the emotional factors that exhaust the sitting worker, make him susceptible to colds, reduce his output, and send him home with a nervous headache. Yes, we get tired because our emotions produce nervous tensions in the body.

The Metropolitan Life Insurance Company pointed that out in a leaflet on fatigue: 'Hard work by itself,' says this great life-insurance company, 'seldom causes fatigue which cannot be cured by a good sleep or rest.... Worry, tenseness, and emotional upsets are three of the biggest causes of fatigue. Often they are to blame when physical or mental work seems to be the cause.... Remember that a tense muscle is a working muscle. Ease up! Save energy for important duties.' Stop now, right where you are, and give yourself a check-up. As you read these lines, are you scowling at the book? Do you feel a strain between the eyes? Are you sitting relaxed in your chair? Or are you hunching up your shoulders? Are the muscles of your face tense? Unless your entire body is as limp and relaxed as an old rag doll, you are at this very moment producing nervous tensions and muscular tensions. You are producing nervous tensions and nervous fatigue! Why do we produce these unnecessary tensions in doing mental work?

Josselyn says: 'I find that the chief obstacle ... is the almost universal belief that hard work requires a feeling of effort, else it is not well done.' So we scowl when we concentrate. We hunch up our shoulders. We call on our muscles to make the motion of effort, which in no way assists our brain in its work. Here is an astonishing and tragic truth: millions of people who wouldn't dream of wasting dollars go right on wasting and squandering their energy with the recklessness of seven drunken sailors in Singapore.

What is the answer to this nervous fatigue? Relax! Relax! Relax! Learn to relax while you are doing your work! Easy? No. You will probably have to reverse the habits of a lifetime. But it is worth the effort, for it may revolutionise your life! Tension is a habit. Relaxing is a habit. And bad habits can be broken, good habits formed.

How do you relax? Do you start with your mind, or do you start with your nerves? You don't start with either. You always begin to relax with your muscles! Let's give it a try. To show how it is done, suppose we start with your eyes. Read this paragraph through, and when you've reached the end, lean back, close your eyes, and say to your eyes silently: "Let go. Let go. Stop straining, stop frowning. Let go. Let go. Repeat that over and over very slowly for a minute.... Didn't you notice that after a few seconds the muscles of the eyes began to obey? Didn't you feel as though some hand had wiped away the tension? Well, incredible as it seems, you have sampled in that one minute the whole key and secret to the art of relaxing. You can do the same thing with the jaw, with the muscles of the face, with the neck, with the shoulders, the whole of the body. But the most important organ of all is the eye. Dr Edmund Jacobson of the University of Chicago has gone so far as to say that if you can completely relax the muscles of the eyes, you can forget all your troubles! The reason the eyes are so important in relieving nervous tension is that they burn up one-fourth of all the nervous energies consumed by the body. That is also why so many people with perfectly sound vision suffer from 'eyestrain'. They are tensing the eyes.

Vicki Baum, the famous novelist, says that when she was a child, she met an old man who taught her one of the most important lessons she ever learned. She had fallen down and cut her knees and hurt her wrist. The old man picked her up; he had once been a circus clown; and, as he brushed her off, he said: 'The reason you injured yourself was because you don't know how to relax. You have to pretend you are as limp as a sock, as an old crumpled sock. Come, I'll show you how to do it.' That old man taught Vicki Baum and the other children how to fall, how to do flip-flops, and how to turn somersaults. And always he insisted: 'Think of yourself as an old crumpled sock. Then you've got to relax!'

You can relax in odd moments, almost anywhere you are. Only don't make an effort to relax. Relaxation is the absence of all tension and effort. Think ease and relaxation. Begin by thinking relaxation of the muscles of your eyes and your face, saying over and over: "Let go ... let go ... let go and relax." Feel the energy flowing out of your facial muscles to the centre of your body. Think of yourself as free from tension as a baby.

Here are five suggestions that will help you learn to relax:

1. Read one of the best books ever written on this subject: *Release from Nervous Tension*, by Dr David Harold Fink.
2. Relax in odd moments. Let your body go limp like an old sock. I keep an old, maroon-coloured sock on my desk as I work—keep it there as a reminder of how limp I ought to be. If you haven't got a sock, a cat will do. Did you ever pick up a kitten sleeping in the sunshine? If so, both ends sagged like a wet newspaper. Even the yogis in India say that if you want to master the art of relaxation, study the cat. I never saw a tired cat, a cat with a nervous breakdown, or a cat suffering from insomnia, worry, or stomach ulcers. You will probably avoid these disasters if you learn to relax as the cat does.
3. Work, as much as possible, in a comfortable position. Remember that tensions in the body

produce aching shoulders and nervous fatigue.
4. Check yourself four or five times a day, and say to yourself: 'Am I making my work harder than it actually is? Am I using muscles that have nothing to do with the work I am doing?' This will help you form the habit of relaxing, and as Dr David Harold Fink says: "Among those who know psychology best, it is habits two to one."
5. Test yourself again at the end of the day, by asking yourself: 'Just how tired am I? If I am tired, it is not because of the mental work I have done but because of the way I have done it.'

'I measure my accomplishments,' says Daniel W. Josselyn, 'not by how tired I am at the end of the day, but how tired I am not.' He says: 'When I feel particularly tired at the end of the day, or when irritability proves that my nerves are tired, I know beyond question that it has been an inefficient day both as to quantity and quality.' If every business man would learn that same lesson, the death rate from 'hypertension' diseases would drop overnight. And we would stop filling up our sanatoriums and asylums with men who have been broken by fatigue and worry.

.21.

Henry Thomas Hamblin

Within You Is the Power

In this section, the author speaks about overcoming limitations and tapping into one's unbound potential. This can be achieved by transmuting negative thoughts into positive affirmations and establishing a nurturing relationship with our spiritual selves.

~

Limitations can be overcome through a realization of Truth. When we say this it is taken for granted that every effort will be made on the physical plane. It is necessary to bathe, exercise and breathe fresh air in order to be well: it is equally necessary to work hard and to give the best of which we are capable, in service, in exchange for that which we receive in the way of supply if we are to be successful. If you keep a gardener, you must pay him. The money that you pay him is part of what you have earned by the sweat of your brain. Therefore you exchange the work of your brain for the labour of his hands, and you are mutually helped and helpful to one another, both giving and receiving, and each one serving life according to his ability. Taking all this for granted, we will pass on to the metaphysical side of our subject. This, by the way, is vastly more important, but the outer, practical work is indispensable nevertheless.

In order to overcome limitations it is necessary to know the Truth and to live in the consciousness of It. For instance, if ill-health is our limitation, then, in order to become free it is necessary that we live in the consciousness of the Wholeness of God and His Divine Idea. If our limitation be restricted means, it is necessary that we live in the consciousness of the inexhaustible and unlimited nature of the Substance from which the Creator brings everything into manifestation. If our limitation is disharmony and unhappiness, then we must become attuned to the Divine harmony in such a way and to such an extent as to cause it to be reflected into the outward life. No matter what our limitation may be, we can find liberation and deliverance by looking to our Divine Source, realizing that in the Perfect Reality all our wants are supplied, and then living in the consciousness of this truth.

Ill-health is, apart from physical causes, an outward sign of an inward warfare or disharmony, caused by wrong thoughts, emotions, beliefs and attitude of mind and soul towards life and God. In other words, the life is lived in an 'error' consciousness of disease and sickness. First, the inward life has to be adjusted in such a way as to harmonize with the laws of our own being and the Divine purpose of life. There must be an inward surrender to the love principle, after which the thoughts must be brought under control so that health-destroying emotions may no longer impair the health. Further, the whole consciousness must, as often as possible, be raised to a realization of the perfect wholeness, which is the reality. If this course is persevered with, a consciousness of health and wholeness becomes a permanent mental state, with the result that health becomes manifested in the life. The outward life is always a reflection or external manifestation of what we are within, or our state of consciousness. Therefore everything depends upon which kind of consciousness it is in which we live.

One who lives in the mental atmosphere of Divine Wholeness, health, and harmony, unconsciously directs all the inner forces of nature into health channels. On the other hand, one who lives in a mental atmosphere of ill-health, as sick and unhealthy people very often do, unconsciously directs all his sub-conscious activities in such a way as to produce sickness and disease.

Again, with regard to lack of means, this state also can be overcome, spiritually, only by living in a higher consciousness of abundance and sufficiency. This affects, unconsciously, every action in such a way as to bring about a better state of affairs. On the other hand, one who lives in a mental atmosphere of limitation and lack, unconsciously directs all his actions towards the production, in his life, of penury and restricted means.

The same rule applies, no matter what the limitations of one's life may be. Freedom can be gained only by realizing the truth about life and being. When we realize the truth, live in the consciousness of it, and become obedient to the laws of life and being, the life becomes increasingly free. This does not mean that if we are plain of feature, and of a stumpy figure, that we shall become beautiful and graceful;

but it does mean that these so-called drawbacks will no longer fetter us and that others will see in us something far better than mere regularity of feature and beauty of form. When the soul is *alive* and the life filled with love, the homeliest face becomes attractive. Neither does it mean that we shall not suffer bereavements and sorrows, difficulties and adversities, but it does mean that we shall cease intensifying these things and creating further troubles by taking life's discipline in the wrong spirit. It also means that we shall be able to overcome all life's difficulties and trials, become a conqueror in the strife, and, in so doing, build up character. Thus the storms of life, instead of destroying us, can succeed only in *making us stronger*. Thus our fate depends not on the storms of life, but upon how we meet them. If we give in to them, or, thinking that they are evil and not a necessary discipline, rebel against them and resist them, then we become shipwrecked on a desolate shore. If, however, we are armed with the knowledge of truth we can set our sails in such a way as to compel the storms of life actually to help us towards the desired haven.

The first step in the direction of knowledge of the truth is right thinking. Every negative thought must be transmuted into its positive opposite, for instance, hate and dislike into love and goodwill, fear into confident trust, poverty into abundance, evil into absolute good, and so on. This will be found to be not easy, but it is possible, and the power to control one's thoughts increases if one perseveres continually, with the passing of the years. A beginner cannot, naturally, expect to be able to exercise the same control as one who has been perseveringly seeking self-mastery for years, but he can make substantial progress and learn from day to day.

The result of thinking in this way is surprising. The reversal of thought may appear at first to be simplicity itself and to lead nowhere in particular, but after a time the vastness of the subject becomes almost appalling. The cultivation and practice of right thinking gradually lead to a knowledge of the Truth. Not an intellectual knowledge of truth, but a realization, by the soul, of *the* Truth. This is the knowing of the Truth which sets men free. We can then look through all the ages and know that all is well. The heavy burden which has oppressed us so long, rolls from our shoulders, and we become free.

AROUSING INWARD POWERS

Man is heir to wonderful and illimitable powers, but until he becomes aware of them and consciously identifies himself with them, they lie dormant and unexpressed, and might just as well not exist at all as far as their use to man, in his unawakened state, is concerned. When, however, man becomes awakened to the great truth that he is a spiritual being: when he learns that the little petty self and finite personality are not his real self at all, but merely a mask to the real man: when he realizes that the Spiritual Ego, a true Divine Spark of, or branch or twig of the Eternal Logos, is *his real Self*: when he understands that his body is not himself, that his mind is not himself, that even his soul is not himself, being but vehicles through which he seeks expression, but that he is spirit, deathless, diseaseless, eternal, forming an integral part of the One Spirit and being identical with It, he enters a new life of almost boundless power.

'I am the Vine, ye are the branches,' said Jesus.

It is unwise to engage in any mystical practices in an attempt to 'force' development and unfoldment. Mystic trances are highly dangerous and are also unnecessary. Psychic experiences and the awakening of psychic centres are also dangerous and lead away from our goal. Breathing exercises, whose object is to awaken inward powers, are *highly dangerous* and are to be condemned in consequence. The cultivation of negative passivity such as inhibiting all thought and making oneself quite passive and open to any influence, is also highly dangerous and should be strictly avoided.

In place of all these unwise practices a short time should be set aside each night and also morning, if possible, for getting into touch with Reality. You should then endeavour to realize that the body, mind, and soul are but vehicles of expression, mere servants of the true Self or Ego. This will bring about in time, a consciousness of identity with the One Eternal Spirit. What Jesus called 'our Father in Heaven'.

One might proceed after this fashion:

My body is not myself, but is merely something that enables me to live this material life and gain experience.

My mind is not myself, but merely an instrument which I use and which obeys my will.

My soul is not myself, but merely a garment of my spirit.

My will is not myself, but is something of which I, the true Self, make use.'

And so on. By this means you gradually approach the great truth which cannot be put into words and which can only become yours through realization or inward spiritual understanding.

In addition one can use a positive statement of Truth, reverently, but with full confidence, such as: 'I am a branch in the True Vine'.

In course of time you will become possessed of a feeling of tremendous and unlimited power and security. This is a great responsibility for this power must be used only in service and not for selfish purposes. If it is used for the acquisition of wealth and the gaining of temporal power, great disaster will be the inevitable result. Yet, if used aright, it is bound to have a great, though unconscious, influence for good on the life, and for this, you are not responsible. Constantly endeavour to serve and bless others, then, because you do not seek them, crowds of blessings will come into your life unbidden, great happiness being one of the chief. Having found the kingdom of heaven it will be your experience that all needed good will be added unto you.

This power may also be used to strengthen character, to overcome in the conflicts of the soul, and to build up the spiritual body which will be our vehicle of expression in higher realms.

SECTION IV

MAKING USE OF OPPORTUNITIES

.22.

Ralph Waldo Emerson

Circles

Published in 1941, Circles is an essay by celebrated American essayist, poet, and pioneer of the Transcendentalist Movement, Ralph Waldo Emerson. Here the author talks about the pursuit of knowledge being the key to self-discovery and embracing new experiences as the only way to escape the mundane repetitiveness of everyday life.

~

The eye is the first circle; the horizon which it forms is the second; and throughout nature this primary picture is repeated without end. It is the highest emblem in the cipher of the world. St. Augustine described the nature of God as a circle whose centre was everywhere and its circumference nowhere. We are all our lifetime reading the copious sense of this first of forms. One moral we have already deduced in considering the circular or compensatory character of every human action. Another analogy we shall now trace, that every action admits of being outdone. Our life is an apprenticeship to the truth that around every circle another can be drawn; that there is no end in nature, but every end is a beginning; that there is always another dawn risen on mid-noon, and under every deep a lower deep opens.

This fact, as far as it symbolizes the moral fact of the Unattainable, the flying Perfect, around which the hands of man can never meet, at once the inspirer and the condemner of every success, may conveniently serve us to connect many illustrations of human power in every department.

There are no fixtures in nature. The universe is fluid and volatile. Permanence is but a word of degrees. Our globe seen by God is a transparent law, not a mass of facts. The law dissolves the fact and holds its fluid. Our culture is the predominance of an idea which draws after it all this train of cities and institutions. Let us rise into another idea; they will disappear. The Greek sculpture is all melted away, as if it had been statues of ice: here and there a solitary figure or fragment remaining, as we see flecks and scraps of snow left in cold dells and mountain clefts in June and July. For the genius that created it creates now somewhat else. The Greek letters last a little longer, but are already passing under the same sentence and tumbling into the inevitable pit which the creation of new thought opens for all that is old. The new continents are built out of the ruins of an old planet; the new races fed out of the decomposition of the foregoing. New arts destroy the old. See the investment of capital in aqueducts, made useless by hydraulics; fortifications, by gunpowder; roads and canals, by railways; sails, by steam; steam, by electricity.

You admire this tower of granite, weathering the hurts of so many ages. Yet a little waving hand built this huge wall, and that which builds is better than that which is built. The hand that built can topple it down much faster. Better than the hand and nimbler was the invisible thought which wrought through it; and thus ever, behind the coarse effect, is a fine cause, which, being narrowly seen, is itself the effect of a finer cause. Everything looks permanent until its secret is known. A rich estate appears to women and children a firm and lasting fact; to a merchant, one easily created out of any materials, and easily lost. An orchard, good tillage, good grounds, seem a fixture, like a gold mine, or a river, to a citizen; but to a large farmer, not much more fixed than the state of the crop. Nature looks provokingly stable and secular, but it has a cause like all the rest; and when once I comprehend that, will these fields stretch so immovably wide, these leaves hang so individually considerable? Permanence is a word of degrees. Everything is medial. Moons are no more bounds to spiritual power than bat-balls.

The key to every man is his thought. Sturdy and defying though he look, he has a helm which he obeys, which is the idea after which all his facts are classified. He can only be reformed by showing him a new idea which commands his own. The life of man is a self-evolving circle, which, from a ring imperceptibly small, rushes on all sides outwards to new and larger circles, and that without end. The extent to which this generation of circles, wheel without wheel, will go, depends on the force or truth of the individual soul. For it is the inert effort of each thought, having formed itself into a circular wave of circumstance, as for instance an empire, rules of an art, a local usage, a religious rite, to heap itself on that ridge and to solidify and hem in the life. But if the soul is quick and strong it bursts over that boundary on all sides and expands another orbit on the great deep, which also runs up into a high wave, with attempt again to stop and to bind. But the heart refuses to be imprisoned; in its first and narrowest pulses it already tends outward with a vast force and to immense and innumerable expansions.

Every ultimate fact is only the first of a new series. Every general law only a particular fact of some more general law presently to disclose itself. There is no outside, no inclosing wall, no circumference to us. The man finishes his story—how good! how final! how it puts a new face on all things! He fills the sky. Lo, on the other side rises also a man and draws a circle around the circle we had just pronounced the outline of the sphere. Then already is our first speaker not man, but only a first speaker. His only redress is forthwith to draw a circle outside of his antagonist. And so men do by themselves. The result of to-day, which haunts the mind and cannot be escaped will presently be abridged into a word, and the principle that seemed to explain nature will itself be included as one example of a bolder generalization. In the thought of to-morrow there is a power to upheave all thy creed, all the creeds, all the literatures of the nations, and marshal thee to a heaven which no epic dream has yet depicted. Every man is not so much a workman in the world as he is a suggestion of that he should be. Men walk as prophecies of the next age.

Step by step we scale this mysterious ladder; the steps are actions; the new prospect is power. Every several result is threatened and judged by that which follows. Everyone seems to be contradicted by the new; it is only limited by the new. The new statement is always hated by the old, and, to those dwelling in the old, comes like an abyss of scepticism. But the eye soon gets wonted to it, for the eye and it are effects of one cause; then its innocence and benefit appear, and presently, all its energy spent, it pales and dwindles before the revelation of the new hour.

.23.

James Allen

Out from the Heart

In this excerpt, the author brings to light the direct correlation between the nature of our thoughts and the quality of our life. Beneficial mental frameworks create an atmosphere of bliss and equilibrium while continually encouraging unpleasant feelings thwart our efforts to achieve success.

~

All sin is ignorance. It is a condition of darkness and undevelopment. The wrong thinker and the wrong-doer is in the same position in the school of life as the ignorant pupil in the school of learning. He has yet to learn how to think and act correctly, that is, in accordance with Law. The pupil in learning is not happy so long as he does his lessons wrongly. Likewise, unhappiness cannot be escaped while sin remains unconquered.

Life is a series of lessons. Some are diligent in learning them, and they become pure, wise, and altogether happy. Others are negligent and do not apply themselves. They remain impure, foolish, and unhappy.

Every form of unhappiness springs from a wrong

condition of mind. Happiness is inherent in right conditions of mind. Happiness is mental harmony, unhappiness is mental inharmony. While a man lives in wrong conditions of mind, he will live a wrong life and will suffer continually.

Suffering is rooted in error. Bliss is inherent in enlightenment. There is salvation for man only in the destruction of his own ignorance, error, and self-delusion. Where there are wrong conditions of mind there is bondage and unrest. Where there are right conditions of mind there is freedom and peace.

Here are some of the leading wrong mental conditions and their disastrous effects upon one's life:

1. *Hatred*—which leads to injury, violence, disaster, and suffering.
2. *Lust*—which leads to confusion of intellect, remorse, shame, and wretchedness.
3. *Covetousness*—which leads to fear, unrest, unhappiness, and loss.
4. *Pride*—which leads to disappointment, humiliation, and lack of self-knowledge.
5. *Vanity*—which leads to distress and mortification of spirit.
6. *Condemnation*—which leads to persecution and hatred from others.
7. *Ill-will*—which leads to failures and troubles.
8. *Self-indulgence*—which leads to misery, loss of judgment, grossness, disease, and neglect.
9. *Anger*—which leads to the loss of power and influence.

10. *Desire or Self-slavery*—which leads to grief, folly, sorrow, uncertainty, and loneliness.

The above wrong conditions of mind are merely negations. They are states of darkness and deprivation and not of positive power. Evil is not a power; it is ignorance and misuse of good. The hater is he who has failed to do the lesson of Love correctly, and he suffers in consequence. When he succeeds in doing it rightly, the hatred will have disappeared, and he will see and understand the darkness and impotence of hatred. This is so with every wrong condition.

The following are some of the more important right mental conditions and their beneficial effects upon one's life:

1. *Love*—which leads to gentle conditions, bliss, and blessedness.
2. *Purity*—which leads to intellectual clearness, joy, invincible confidence.
3. *Selflessness*—which leads to courage, satisfaction, happiness, and abundance.
4. *Humility*—which leads to calmness, restfulness, knowledge of Truth.
5. *Gentleness*—which leads to emotional equilibrium, contentment under all circumstances.
6. *Compassion*—which leads to protection, love, and reverence from others.
7. *Goodwill*—which leads to gladness, success.
8. *Self-control*—which leads to peace of mind, true judgment, refinement, health, and honour.
9. *Patience*—which leads to mental power, far-reaching influence.

10. *Self-conquest*—which leads to enlightenment, wisdom, insight, and profound peace.

The above right conditions of mind are states of positive power, light, joyful possession, and knowledge. The good man knows. He has learned to do his lessons correctly and thereby understands the exact proportions which make up the sum of life. He is enlightened, and he knows good and evil. He is supremely happy, doing only that which is divinely right.

The man who is involved in the wrong conditions of mind, does not know. He is ignorant of good and evil, of himself, of the inward causes which make his life. He is unhappy and believes other people are entirely the cause of his unhappiness. He works blindly, and lives in darkness, seeing no central purpose in existence, and no orderly and lawful sequence in the course of things.

He who aspires to the attainment of the Higher Life in its completion—who would perceive with unveiled vision the true order of things and the meaning of life—let him abandon all the wrong conditions of the heart, and persevere unceasingly in the practice of good. If he suffers, or doubts, or is unhappy, let him search within until he finds the cause, and having found it, let him cast it away. Let him so guard and purify his heart that every day less of evil and more of good shall issue therefrom. So he will daily become stronger, nobler, and wiser. So will his blessedness increase, and the Light of Truth, growing ever brighter and brighter within him, will dispel all gloom, and illuminate his Pathway.

.24.

Orison Swett Marden

The Victorious Attitude

In this excerpt from his highly acclaimed book, the author encourages us to voice our deepest desires with confidence, give them the wings to fly, and then watch with content as our dreams transform into reality. The key is to remain steadfast in the pursuit of our ideal and believe in the vision in our heart.

~

All human achievements have been pulled out of the unseen by the brain, through the mind reaching out and fashioning the wealth of material at its disposal into the shapes which matched the wishes, the desires, of the achievers.

All the great discoveries, great inventions, great deeds that have lifted man up from his animal existence have been wrought out of the actual by the perpetual thinking of and visualizing these things by their authors. These grand characters clung to their vision, nursed it until they became mighty magnets that attracted out of the universal intelligence the realization of their dreams.

Most revolutionary inventions have evolved from a flash of thought. The sewing machine, for example, started with a simple idea, which the inventor held persistently in his mind until through his efforts the idea materialized into the concrete reality. Elias Howe used to watch his wife making garments, sewing, sewing far into the night, and it set him thinking, questioning whether such drudgery was really necessary. As he watched her busy needle fly back and forth, he began to wonder if this same work which it took his wife so long to do could not be done with less labour and in half the time by some sort of mechanical contrivance. He kept nursing his idea, thinking what a splendid thing it would be if someone could relieve millions of women from this toil, which frequently had to be done at night after a day of hard work. He began to experiment with crude devices, clinging to his vision through poverty and the denunciation of friends, who thought the man must be crazy to spend his time on 'such a fool idea'. But at last, his vision materialized into a marvellous reality, a perfected machine which has emancipated the women of the world from infinite drudgery.

The idea of the telephone was flashed into the mind of Professor Alexander Bell by the drawing of a string through a hole in the bottom of a tin can, by means of which he found that the voice could be transmitted. The idea took such complete possession of the inventor that it robbed him of sleep and, for a time, made him poor. But nothing could rob him of his vision or prevent him from struggling to work it out of the visionary stage into the actual.

I lived near Professor Bell, in the next room, indeed, while he worked on his invention. I saw much of his struggle with poverty, heard the criticisms and denunciations of his friends, as he persisted in his visionary work until the telephone became a reality—a reality without which modern business could not be conducted.

All of Edison's inventions, those of every inventor, have been wrought out on the same principle that gave us the sewing machine and the telephone. They all started in simple ideas, in dream visions which were nursed and worked into actualities.

According to Darwin, the desire to ascend into the heavens preceded the appearance and development of the eagle's wings. It is said our different organs and functions have been developed from a sense of need of them, just as the wings of the eagle developed from a desire to fly.

The brain cells grow in response to desire. Where there is no desire there is no growth. The brain develops most in the direction of the leading ambition, where the mental activities are the most pronounced. The desire for a musical career, for instance, develops the musical brain cells. Business ambition develops that part of the brain which has to do with business, the cells which are brought into action in executive management, in administering affairs, in money making. Wherever we make our demand upon the brain by desire that part responds in growth.

A poor girl, the daughter of humble people in Maine who thought that to become a public singer was an unforgivable sin, could not in the beginning see any possible way to realize the dreams she held in secret, but she kept visualizing her dream, nursing her desire and doing the only thing for its realization her parents would allow—singing in a little church choir. Gradually the way opened, and one step led to another until the little Maine girl became the famous Madame Nordica, one of the world's greatest singers.

No matter if you are a poor girl away back in the country, and see no possible way of leaving your poor old father and mother in order to prepare for your career, don't let go of your desire. Whether it be music, art, literature, business or a profession, hold to it. No matter how dark the outlook, keep on visualizing your desire and light and opportunity will come to enable you to make it a reality. Whatever the Creator has fitted you to do He will give you a chance to do, if you cling to your vision and struggle as best you can for its attainment.

Think of the Lillian Nordicas, the Lucy Stones, the Louisa Alcotts, the Mary Lyons, the Dr Anna Howard Shaws, the thousands of women who were hedged in just as you are, by poverty or forbidding circumstances of some sort, yet succeeded in spite of everything in doing what they desired to do, in being what they longed to be. Take heart and believe that God has given you also "all implements divine to shape the way" to your soul's desire.

If you are a boy on a farm and feel that you are a born engineer, yet see no possible way to get a technical education, don't lose heart or hope. Get what books you can on your specialty. Cling to your vision. Push out in every direction that is possible to you. It may take years, but if you are true to yourself your concentration on your desire, your pushing toward it, will open a door into the light, and before you know it you will be on the road to your goal.

The Washingtons, the Lincolns, the Faradays, the Edisons, the men who have done most for their country and for humanity have had to struggle as hard as you are struggling to attain their heart's desire. The opportunities for boys and girls to bring out whatever the Creator has implanted in them are ten to one to-day to what they were one hundred, or fifty, or even twenty-five years ago. The great danger in our time is not lack of chance or opportunity but of losing our vision, of letting our ambition die.

Most of us instead of treating our desires seriously trifle with them as though they were only to be played with, as though they never could be realities. We do not believe in their divinity. We regard our heart longings, our soul yearnings as fanciful vagaries, romances of the imagination. Yet we know that every invention, every discovery or achievement that has blessed the world began in a desire, in a longing to produce or to do a certain thing, and that the persistent longing was accompanied by a struggle to make the mental picture a reality.

It is difficult for us to grasp the fact that ambition, accompanied by effort, is actually a creative power which tends to realize itself. Our minds are like that of the doubting disciple, who would not believe that his Lord had risen until he had actually thrust his finger into the side which had been pierced by a cruel spear. Only the things that we see seem real to us when, as a matter of fact, the most real things in the world are the unseen.

We never doubt the existence of the force that brings the bud out of the seed, the foliage and the flower out of the bud, the fruits, the vegetables from the flower. It is invisible. We cannot sense it, but we know that it is mightier than anything we see. No one can see or hear or feel gravitation, or the forces which balance the earth and whirl it with lightning speed through space, bringing it round its orbit without a variation of the tenth of a second in a century, yet who can doubt their reality? Does anyone question the mighty power of electricity because it cannot be seen or heard or smelled?

The potency of our desires, of our soul longings, when backed by the effort to make them realities, is just as real as is that of any of the unseen forces in Nature's great laboratory. The great cosmic ether is packed with invisible potentialities. Whatever comes out of it to you comes in response to your call. Everything you have accomplished in life has been a result of a psychic law which, consciously or unconsciously, you have obeyed.

Do not make the mistake of thinking that the way will not open because you cannot now see any possible means of achieving that for which you long. The very intensity of your longing for a certain career, to do a certain thing, is the best evidence that you have the ability to match it, and that this ability was given you for a purpose, even to play a divine, a magnificent part in the great universal plan. The longing is merely the forerunner of achievement. It is the seed that will germinate if nurtured by effort.

If, however, you stop at sowing the seed you will get just about as much harvest as a farmer would get if he should sow his seeds without preparing the soil, without fertilizing or cultivating it or keeping down the weeds. It is the blending of the practical with the ideal that brings the harvest from the seed thought. You must keep on struggling toward your ideal. No matter how black and forbidding the way ahead of you, just imagine you are carrying a lantern which will advance with you and give light enough for the next step. It is not necessary to see to the end of the road. All the light you need is for the next step. Faith in your vision and persistent endeavour will do the rest. There is no doubt that if we do our part, the Divinity that has created us, given us an appointed place and a work in the plan of the universe, will bring things out better than we can plan or even imagine.

Send out your wishes, cherish your desires, force out your yearnings, your heart longings with all the intensity and persistency you can muster, and you will be surprised to see how soon they will begin to attract their affinities, how they will grow and take tangible shape, and ultimately become actual things. Fling out your desires into the cosmic ether boldly, with the utmost confidence. Therein you will gather the material which shall build into reality the castle of your dreams.

.25.

Neema Majumdar, Nandini Mirani, and Saloni Jhaveri

Finding Meaning in Life with the Bhagavad Gita

In Verse 33, the Bhagavad Gita reveals the path to mastery as one seeped in the application of consistent and sincere efforts. By approaching hardships and failure with compassion, we ensure an environment where everyone can thrive and find their voice.

~

Mastery Through Persistent Effort

अथ चितं समाधातु न शक्रोषि मयि स्थिरम्।
अभ्यासयोगेन ततो मामिच्छाप्तुं धनजय: ||12-9||

atha cittaṁ samādhātuṁ na śaknoṣi mayi sthiram
abhyāsayogena tato māṁ icchāptuṁ dhanañjaya

If you are not able to absorb your mind steadily in Me, Dhananjaya (Arjuna)! then through the practice of yoga may you seek to reach Me. (12.9)

The Gita's wisdom may inspire a resolve to change behaviours or attitudes, but transformations in habitual thought patterns do not happen overnight. Persistent effort is essential to break recurring styles of thinking and responding. Even when we slip up, we need to continue the effort without self-reproach.

When faced with unpleasantness, some people have a chronic habit to let go and not speak up, while others have a tendency to retaliate aggressively. When we remain passive to avoid confrontation, we build up inner resentment, and empower the aggressor. On the other hand, shouting or violence escalates matters. Both these extremes make the situation more complex and require correction. The wise option is to assess each situation and determine whether it calls for our intervention, what is our sphere of influence, and what is the manner in which we can intervene effectively.

Changing established patterns of communication between two people takes commitment, time, and effort. A mother once expressed her inability to stop her daughter from using abusive language towards her. When asked why she had allowed it to continue for so long, she said that she did not want to be firm as her daughter was already going through certain mental and physical challenges. By consistently letting go, the mother had inadvertently magnified her own internal trauma, and the daughter too may have suffered feelings of guilt and sadness following the abuse. A better response would have been to have a conversation with the daughter—not with an intention to reprimand, but to make their relationship healthy and honest.

Convinced that the pattern needed to change, the mother began to consistently and intelligently improve her communication with her daughter. The mother was authentic in expressing what she felt, and at the same time listened to her daughter's viewpoint patiently. Even though difficult initially, they were able to move their relationship to a better level.

A bright manager at a multinational company felt threatened when a colleague from another department was brought in to execute an important project. He resented the attention his colleague was getting from the boss for his experience and execution skills. The manager began to feel incompetent. He grew embittered, and over a period of time, his actions and behaviour became largely influenced by envy and insecurity. This started affecting the group dynamic as well as his own well-being.

At one point the manager realized that his attitude was unsustainable and not serving him in any way. He recognized that his colleague's competencies were clearly talents he valued, as he was impacted by them. He tried to convert his competitiveness into admiration and cooperation. Though not easy in the beginning, with persistent effort, he was able to aim at cultivating his own strengths instead of delving into feelings of inadequacy. Eventually, he was able to develop skills that mattered to him, rather than being weighed down by unproductive thought patterns that were neither serving him, nor conducive to the work environment.

With perseverance, alertness, and deliberate effort (abhyasa), we are able to live our lives with the larger vision of Ishvara. This change in ourselves can even lead to a change in the circumstances around us.

.26.

Joseph Murphy

The Power of Your Subconscious Mind

In this section, the author describes how we are the sum of our thoughts and provides beneficial pointers on creating life-affirming patterns of thinking that allow us to harness the power of the conscious mind and experience joyful living.

~

When you study the cellular system and the structure of the organs, such as eyes, ears, heart, liver, bladder, etc., you learn they consist of groups of cells which form a group intelligence whereby they function together and are able to take orders and carry them out in deductive function at the suggestion of the master mind (conscious mind).

A careful study of the single-celled organism shows you what goes on in your complex body. Though the monocellular organism has no organs, it still gives evidence of mind action and reaction performing the basic functions of movement, alimentation, assimilation, and elimination.

Many say there is an intelligence, which will take care of your body if you let it alone. That is true, but the difficulty is that the conscious mind always interferes with its five-sense evidence based on outer appearances, leading to the sway of false beliefs, fears, and mere opinion. When fear, false beliefs, and negative patterns are made to register in your subconscious mind through psychological, emotional conditioning, there is no other course open to the subconscious mind except to act on the blueprint specifications offered to it.

The Subconscious Mind Works Continually for the Common Good

The subjective self within you works continuously for the general good, reflecting an innate principle of harmony behind all things. Your subconscious mind has its own will, and it is a very real something in itself. It acts night and day whether you act upon it or not. It is the builder of your body, but you cannot see, hear, or feel it building, as all this is a silent process. Your subconscious has a life of its own which is always moving toward harmony, health, and peace. This is the divine norm within it seeking expression through you at all times.

You are the sum total of your own thoughts. You can keep from entertaining negative thought and imagery. The way to get rid of darkness is with light; the way to overcome cold is with heat; the way to overcome the negative thought is to substitute the good thought. Affirm the good, and the bad will vanish.

How Faith in Your Subconscious Powers Makes You Whole

A young man, who came to my lectures on the healing power of the subconscious mind, had severe eye trouble, which his doctor said necessitated an operation. He said to himself, 'My subconscious made my eyes, and it can heal me.'

Each night, as he went to sleep, he entered into a drowsy, meditative state, the condition akin to sleep. His attention was immobilized and focused on the eye doctor. He imagined the doctor was in front of him, and he plainly heard, or imagined he heard, the doctor saying to him, 'A miracle has happened!' He heard this over and over again every night for perhaps five minutes or so before going to sleep. At the end of three weeks, he again went to the ophthalmologist who had previously examined his eyes, and the physician said to this man, 'This is a miracle!' What happened? This man impressed his subconscious mind using the doctor as an instrument or a means of convincing it or conveying the idea. Through repetition, faith, and expectancy he impregnated his subconscious mind. His subconscious mind made his eye; within it was the perfect pattern, and immediately it proceeded to heal the eye. This is another example of how faith in the healing power of your subconscious can make you whole.

Pointers to Review

1. Your subconscious is the builder of your body and is on the job twenty-four hours a day. You interfere with its life-giving patterns by negative thinking.
2. Charge your subconscious with the task of evolving an answer to any problem, prior to sleep and it will answer you.
3. Watch your thoughts. Every thought accepted as true is sent by your brain to your solar plexus—your abdominal brain—and is brought into your world as a reality.
4. Know that you can remake yourself by giving a new blueprint to your subconscious mind.
5. The tendency of your subconscious is always lifeward. Your job is with your conscious mind. Feed your subconscious mind with premises, which are true. Your subconscious is always reproducing according to your habitual mental patterns.
6. You build a new body every eleven months. Change your body by changing your thoughts and keeping them changed.
7. Thoughts of jealousy, fear, worry, and anxiety tear down and destroy your nerves and glands bringing about mental and physical diseases of all kinds.
8. What you affirm consciously and feel as true will be made manifest in your mind, body, and affairs. Affirm the good and enter into the joy of living.

.27.

William George Jordan

The Majesty of Calmness

In his seminal work published in 1900, American essayist and editor William George Jordan empowers readers to reassess their approach to life by viewing it through a simpler lens. This extract talks about the transformative power of doing the best you can, at every given task, at any moment of the day—a humble choice that will illuminate the path to fulfilment.

~

Life is a wondrously complex problem for the individual, until, someday, in a moment of illumination, he awakens to the great realization that he can make it simple—never quite simple, but always simpler. There are a thousand mysteries of right and wrong that have baffled the wise men of the ages. There are depths in the great fundamental questions of the human race that no plummet of philosophy has ever sounded. There are wild cries of honest hunger for truth that seek to pierce the silence beyond the grave, but to them ever echo back—only a repetition of their unanswered cries.

To us all, comes, at times, the great note of questioning despair that darkens our horizon and paralyzes our effort:

'If there really be a God, if eternal justice really rule the world,' we say, 'why should life be as it is? Why do some men starve while others feast; why does virtue often languish in the shadow while vice triumphs in the sunshine; why does failure so often dog the footsteps of honest effort, while the success that comes from trickery and dishonour is greeted with the world's applause? How is it that the loving father of one family is taken by death, while the worthless incumbrance of another is spared? Why is there so much unnecessary pain, sorrowing and suffering in the world—why, indeed, should there be any?'

Neither philosophy nor religion can give any final satisfactory answer that is capable of logical demonstration, of absolute proof. There is ever, even after the best explanations, a residuum of the unexplained. We must then fall back in the eternal arms of faith, and be wise enough to say, 'I will not be disconcerted by these problems of life, I will not permit them to plunge me into doubt, and to cloud my life with vagueness and uncertainty. Man arrogates much to himself when he demands from the Infinite the full solution of all His mysteries. I will found my life on the impregnable rock of a simple fundamental truth—This glorious creation with its millions of wondrous phenomena pulsing ever in harmony with eternal law must have a Creator, that Creator must be omniscient and omnipotent. But that Creator Himself cannot, in justice, demand of any creature more than the best that that individual can give.'

I will do each day, in every moment, the best I can by the light I have; I will ever seek more light, more perfect illumination of truth, and ever live as best I can in harmony with the truth as I see it. If failure comes I will meet it bravely; if my pathway then lie in the shadow of trial, sorrow and suffering, I shall have the restful peace and the calm strength of one who has done his best, who can look back upon the past with no pang of regret, and who has heroic courage in facing the results, whatever they be, knowing that he could not make them different."

Upon this life-plan, this foundation, man may erect any superstructure of religion or philosophy that he conscientiously can erect; he should add to his equipment for living every shred of strength and inspiration, moral, mental or spiritual that is in his power to secure. This simple working faith is opposed to no creed, is a substitute for none; it is but a primary belief, a citadel, a refuge where the individual can retire for strength when the battle of life grows hard.

A mere theory of life, that remains but a theory, is about as useful to a man, as a gilt-edged menu is to a starving sailor on a raft in mid-ocean. It is irritating but not stimulating. No rule for higher living will help a man in the slightest, until he reaches out and appropriates it for himself, until he make it practical in his daily life, until that seed of theory in his mind blossom into a thousand flowers of thought and word and act.

If a man honestly seeks to live his best at all times, that determination is visible in every moment of his living, no trifle in his life can be too insignificant to reflect his principle of living. The sun illuminates and beautifies a fallen leaf by the roadside as impartially as a towering mountain peak in the Alps. Every drop of water in the ocean is an epitome of the chemistry of the whole ocean; every drop is subject to precisely the same laws as dominate the united infinity of billions of drops that make that miracle of Nature, men call the Sea. No matter how humble the calling of the individual, how uninteresting and dull the round of his duties, he should do his best. He should dignify what he is doing by the mind he puts into it, he should vitalize what little he has of power or energy or ability or opportunity, in order to prepare himself to be equal to higher privileges when they come. This will never lead man to that weak content that is satisfied with whatever falls to his lot. It will rather fill his mind with that divine discontent that cheerfully accepts the best—merely as a temporary substitute for something better.

The man who is seeking ever to do his best is the man who is keen, active, wide-awake, and aggressive. He is ever watchful of himself in trifles; his standard is not 'What will the world say?' but 'Is it worthy of me?'

Edwin Booth, one of the greatest actors on the American stage, would never permit himself to assume an ungraceful attitude, even in his hours of privacy. In this simple thing, he ever lived his best. On the stage every move was one of unconscious grace. Those of his company who were conscious of their motions were the awkward ones, who were seeking in public to undo or to conceal the carelessness of the gestures and motions of their private life. The man who is slipshod and thoughtless in his daily speech, whose vocabulary is a collection of anæmic commonplaces, whose repetitions of phrases and extravagance of interjections act but as feeble disguises to his lack of ideas, will never be brilliant on an occasion when he longs to outshine the stars. Living at one's best is constant preparation for instant use. It can never make one overprecise, self-conscious, affected, or priggish. Education, in its highest sense, is *conscious* training of mind or body to act *unconsciously*. It is conscious formation of mental habits, not mere acquisition of information.

One of the many ways in which the individual unwisely eclipses himself, is in his worship of the fetich of luck. He feels that all others are lucky, and that whatever he attempts, fails. He does not realize the untiring energy, the unremitting concentration, the heroic courage, the sublime patience that is the secret of some men's success. Their "luck" was that they had prepared themselves to be equal to their opportunity when it came and were awake to recognize it and receive it. His own opportunity came and departed unnoted; it would not waken him from his dreams of some untold wealth that would fall into his lap. So he grows discouraged and envies those whom he should emulate, and he bandages his arm and chloroforms his energies, and performs his duties in a perfunctory way, or he passes through life, just ever 'sampling' lines of activity.

The honest, faithful struggler should always realize that failure is but an episode in a true man's life—never the whole story. It is never easy to meet, and no philosophy can make it so, but the steadfast courage to master conditions, instead of complaining of them, will help him on his way; it will ever enable him to get the best out of what he has. He never knows the long series of vanquished failures that give solidity to someone else's success; he does not realize the price that some rich man, the innocent football of political malcontents and demagogues, has heroically paid for wealth and position.

The man who has a pessimist's doubt of all things; who demands a certified guarantee of his future; whoever fears his work will not be recognized or appreciated; or that after all, it is really not worthwhile, will never live his best. He is dulling his capacity for real progress by his hypnotic course of excuses for inactivity, instead of a strong tonic of reasons for action.

One of the most weakening elements in the individual make-up is the surrender to the oncoming of years. Man's self-confidence dims and dies in the fear of age. 'This new thought,' he says of some suggestion tending to higher development, 'is good; it is what we need. I am glad to have it for my children; I would have been happy to have had some such help when I was at school, but it is too late for me. I am a man advanced in years.'

This is but blind closing of life to wondrous possibilities. The knell of lost opportunity is never tolled in this life. It is never too late to recognize truth and to live by it. It requires only greater effort, closer attention, deeper consecration; but the impossible does not exist for the man who is self-confident and is willing to pay the price in time and struggle for his success or development. Later in life, the assessments are heavier in progress, as in life insurance, but that matters not to that mighty self-confidence that *will* not grow old while knowledge can keep it young.

Socrates, when his hair whitened with the snow of age, learned to play on instruments of music. Cato, at fourscore, began his study of Greek, and the same age saw Plutarch beginning, with the enthusiasm of a boy, his first lessons in Latin. *The Character of Man*, Theophrastus' greatest work, was begun on his ninetieth birthday. Chaucer's Canterbury Tales was the work of the poet's declining years. Ronsard, the father of French poetry, whose sonnets even translation cannot destroy, did not develop his poetic faculty until nearly fifty. Benjamin Franklin at this age had just taken his really first steps of importance in philosophic pursuits. Arnauld, the theologian and sage, translated Josephus in his eightieth year. Winckelmann, one of the most famous writers on classic antiquities, was the son of a shoemaker, and lived in obscurity and ignorance until the prime of life. Hobbes, the English philosopher, published his version of the Odyssey in his eighty-seventh year, and his Iliad one year later. Chevreul, the great French scientist, whose untiring labours in the realm of colour have so enriched the world, was busy, keen and active when Death called him, at the age of 103.

These men did not fear age; these few names from the great muster-roll of the famous ones who defied the years, should be voices of hope and heartening to every individual whose courage and confidence are weak. The path of truth, higher living, truer development in every phase of life, is never shut from the individual—until he closes it himself. Let man feel this, believe it and make this faith a real and living factor in his life and there are no limits to his progress. He has but to live his best at all times, and rest calm and untroubled no matter what results come to his efforts. The constant looking backward to what might have been, instead of forward to what may be, is a great weakener of self-confidence. This worry for the old past, this wasted energy, for that which no power in the world can restore, ever lessens the individual's faith in himself, weakens his efforts to develop himself for the future to the perfection of his possibilities.

Nature in her beautiful love and tenderness, says to man, weakened and worn and weary with the struggle, 'Do in the best way you can the trifle that is under your hand at this moment; do it in the best spirit of preparation for the future your thought suggests; bring all the light of knowledge from all the past to aid you. Do this and you have done your best. The past is forever closed to you. It is closed forever to you. No worry, no struggle, no suffering, no agony of despair can alter it. It is as much beyond your power as if it were a million years of eternity behind you. Turn all that past, with its sad hours, weakness and sin, its wasted opportunities as light; in confidence and hope, upon the future. Turn it all in fuller truth and light so as to make each trifle of this present a new past it will be a joy to look back to; each trifle a grander, nobler, and more perfect preparation for the future. The present and the future you can make from it is yours; the past has gone back, with all its messages, all its history, all its records to the God who loaned you the golden moments to use in obedience to His law.'

.28.

Kahlil Gibran

The Prophet

In this section, the Prophet tell us about the infinite nature of time. No matter how much one wants to direct the course of its flow, time remains immeasurable. All we must strive to do is remember the past with compassion and look towards the future with wishful desire and excitement.

~

On Time

And an astronomer said, Master, what of Time?
And he answered:
You would measure time the measureless and the immeasurable.
You would adjust your conduct and even direct the course of your spirit according to hours and seasons.
Of time you would make a stream upon whose bank you would sit and watch its flowing.
Yet the timeless in you is aware of life's timelessness,
And knows that yesterday is but today's memory and tomorrow is today's dream.

And that that which sings and contemplates in you is still dwelling within the bounds of that first moment which scattered the stars into space. Who among you does not feel that his power to love is boundless?

And yet who does not feel that very love, though boundless, encompassed within the centre of his being, and moving not from love thought to love thought, nor from love deeds to other love deeds?

And is not time even as love is, undivided and paceless?

But if in your thought you must measure time into seasons, let each season encircle all the other seasons,
And let today embrace the past with remembrance and the future with longing.

Notes on Contributors

Arnold Bennett was a celebrated English novelist, playwright, and essayist, acclaimed for his diverse literary contributions that captured the essence of early twentieth-century society. His novels, including *The Old Wives' Tale*, *The Grand Babylon Hotel*, and the *Clayhanger* trilogy, showcased vivid realism and his acute observation of human nature, social dynamics, and the impact of modernity. Bennett's stories delved into the lives of ordinary characters, depicting their varied aspirations, challenges, and growth. As a chronicler of the times, he captured the transformations occurring in society during the transition from the Victorian era to the modern age. He died in 1931.

Arthur Schopenhauer was a German philosopher best known for his 1818 publication, *The World as Will and Representation*. Schopenhauer's philosophy often delved into transcending individual desires to escape the cycles of inherent suffering in the world through contemplation, aesthetics, and asceticism. Schopenhauer's ideas significantly influenced later philosophers, particularly Friedrich Nietzsche and Jean-Paul Sartre. His unique perspective on the human condition continues to stimulate debates about the nature of existence, the role of suffering, and the potential for attaining liberation from the endless cycle of want. He died in 1860.

Dale Carnegie was an American author and lecturer. He was born in poverty in Missouri in 1888. A skilful orator from a young age, Carnegie was active in his school debate team. He won several intercollegiate public speaking contests. He started his career as a salesman upon graduating from college in 1908. Following a brief stint as an actor in 1911, he taught his first public speaking course at the YMCA in New York. His courses soon became immensely popular and, by 1930, he began recruiting individuals to deliver courses in professional improvement throughout the country. He is considered a pioneer in self-improvement and his works including *How to Win Friends and Influence People* (1936) and *How to Stop Worrying and Start Living* (1948) are popular to this day. He died in 1955.

Henry Thomas Hamblin was a prominent British author and spiritual teacher known for his everlasting contributions to the New Thought Movement. His influential writings highlighted the power of positive thinking, self-discovery, and the alignment of one's thoughts with their desired reality. Hamblin's most renowned work, *The Power of Thought*, was published in 1921 and is today considered a cornerstone in the field of personal development and spiritual growth. He believed in the inherent potential of individuals to shape their destinies through the mastery of their minds. Hamblin's teachings offered profound yet practical insights into harnessing the creative force of thoughts, continuing to inspire millions on their journeys of self-improvement. He died in 1958.

James Allen was born in 1864 to a working-class family in Leicester, England. Following the death of his father, he was forced to find work to support his family at the age of fifteen. Throughout the 1890s he worked as a secretary in a British manufacturing firm and later found a role in journalism. In 1898, he explored his interest in spirituality by writing for a magazine called the *Herald of the Golden Age*, and by 1902, he started his publication called *The Epoch*. *As a Man Thinketh*, published in 1903, is his third and most famous work. After retiring in 1903, he lived in a small town in North Devon with his wife, Lily, and daughter, Nora, and continued writing until his death in 1912.

Joseph Murphy was born in Ireland in 1898. He joined the Jesuits at an early age and began preparing to be initiated into the priesthood. However, he then decided to emigrate to America and became a pharmacist in New York City. He was interested in the study of different religions and travelled to India to learn about Asian religions. He later started his church in Los Angeles in the 1940s. He earned a PhD in psychology from the University of South California and wrote thirty books in the self-help genre. *The Power of Your Subconscious Mind*, which was published in 1963, is his most famous work. He died in 1981.

Kahlil Gibran is a revered Lebanese-American poet, philosopher, and visual artist, celebrated for his introspective writing that poetically captures complex emotions and explores universal truths surrounding the human experience. His magnum opus, *The Prophet*, published in 1923, encapsulates his wisdom on life's fundamental aspects, such as love, pain, joy, and freedom. Gibran's poetic language and spiritual insights have resonated across generations, inviting readers to contemplate the deeper meaning of existence. His words reflect a melange of his Eastern heritage and Western influences, creating a harmonious blend of mysticism and modernity that greatly appeal to those seeking enlightenment. He died in 1931.

Nandini Mirani has an MBA in finance from Boston University and has worked in consulting, paper, and social impact industries. She serves as an active trustee of the non-profit Muljibhai Patel Urological Hospital (MPUH). Outside of this role, she combines her study of Vedanta with her passion for reading and writing.

Napoleon Hill was an American motivational author. He was born in Virginia in 1883 and started writing at the age of thirteen. He is most famous for his work *Think and Grow Rich*, an all-time bestseller published in 1937. He established the Napoleon Hill Foundation, a non-profit institution that promotes his philosophy of personal achievement, leadership, and success. He died in 1970.

Neema Majmudar has a master's degree in International Affairs from the School of International and Public

Affairs (SIPA), Columbia University. She has studied the Upanishads, Bhagavad Gita, and Sanskrit with Swami Dayananda Saraswati. She worked for almost twenty years at the United Nations, before becoming a full-time teacher of Vedanta and the Gita. Neema and her husband, Surya Tahora, conduct regular workshops and retreats on Vedanta.

Orison Swett Marden was a prominent American author and inspirational speaker whose writings have influenced countless people, from the common reader to presidents and business magnates. His teachings centre on personal development, the principles of success, and the power of a positive mindset. Marden's influential books, *Pushing to the Front* and *An Iron Will*, offered hands-on advice on achieving goals and overcoming obstacles through determination and self-discipline. It is believed Marden's work laid the foundation for the self-help genre, inspiring generations to tap into their inner potential and lead fulfilling lives. He died in 1924.

Ralph Waldo Emerson was a renowned American essayist, philosopher, poet, and central figure in the Transcendentalist Movement of the nineteenth century. His thought-provoking essays, including *Self-reliance* and *Nature,* advocated for individualism, self-expression, and a deeper connection to the natural world. At the core of his writings was the belief that individuals have inherent wisdom and should trust their intuition. He encouraged people to break away from the rigidities of societal institutions and discover their true selves. His philosophical contributions left an indelible mark on American literature, later influencing Henry David Thoreau and Walt Whitman. He died in 1882.

Saloni Jhaveri has an AB in economics from Barnard College. She co-founded and ran a software company for twenty-two years. She has been involved with the Times Litfest as a curator for children's events. She enjoys her varied pursuits including nutrition, philosophy, reading, yoga, and travel.

William George Jordan was a distinguished American essayist, editor, lecturer, and a notable figure in the development of self-improvement as a genre of literature. He was renowned for his extensive work on personal growth, psychology, and leadership. He rose to prominence with books such as *The Majesty of Calmness* and *The Kingship of Self-control,* where he emphasized the significance of inner calm, self-discipline, and ethical living in a fast-paced world. He championed the idea that true strength lies in mastering one's thoughts and emotions. He died in 1928.